Cloud Service Provider
Complete Self-Assessment Guide

The guidance in this Self-Assessment is based on Cloud Service Provider best practices and standards in business process architecture, design and quality management. The guidance is also based on the professional judgment of the individual collaborators listed in the Acknowledgments.

Notice of rights

Copyright © by The Art of Service
http://theartofservice.com
service@theartofservice.com

Table of Contents

About The Art of Service

The Art of Service, Business Process Architects since 2000, is dedicated to helping stakeholders achieve excellence.

Defining, designing, creating, and implementing a process to solve a stakeholders challenge or meet an objective is the most valuable role... In EVERY group, company, organization and department.

Unless you're talking a one-time, single-use project, there should be a process. Whether that process is managed and implemented by humans, AI, or a combination of the two, it needs to be designed by someone with a complex enough perspective to ask the right questions.

Someone capable of asking the right questions and step back and say, 'What are we really trying to accomplish here? And is there a different way to look at it?'

With The Art of Service's Standard Requirements Self-Assessments, we empower people who can do just that — whether their title is marketer, entrepreneur, manager, salesperson, consultant, Business Process Manager, executive assistant, IT Manager, CIO etc... —they are the people who rule the future. They are people who watch the process as it happens, and ask the right questions to make the process work better.

Contact us when you need any support with this Self-Assessment and any help with templates, blue-prints and examples of standard documents you might need:

http://theartofservice.com
service@theartofservice.com

Acknowledgments

This checklist was developed under the auspices of The Art of Service, chaired by Gerardus Blokdyk.

Representatives from several client companies participated in the preparation of this Self-Assessment.

In addition, we are thankful for the design and printing services provided.

Included Resources - how to access

Included with your purchase of the book is the Cloud Service Provider Self-Assessment Spreadsheet Dashboard which contains all questions and Self-Assessment areas and auto-generates insights, graphs, and project RACI planning - all with examples to get you started right away.

How? Simply send an email to
access@theartofservice.com
with this books' title in the subject to get the Cloud Service Provider Self Assessment Tool right away.

You will receive the following contents with New and Updated specific criteria:

• The latest quick edition of the book in PDF

• The latest complete edition of the book in PDF, which criteria correspond to the criteria in...

• The Self-Assessment Excel Dashboard, and...

• Example pre-filled Self-Assessment Excel Dashboard to get familiar with results generation

• In-depth specific Checklists covering the topic

• Project management checklists and templates to assist with implementation

INCLUDES LIFETIME SELF ASSESSMENT UPDATES

Every self assessment comes with Lifetime Updates and Lifetime Free Updated Books. Lifetime Updates is an industry-first feature which allows you to receive verified self assessment updates, ensuring you always have the most accurate information at your fingertips.

Get it now- you will be glad you did - do it now, before you forget.

Send an email to **access@theartofservice.com** with this books' title in the subject to get the Cloud Service Provider Self Assessment Tool right away.

Your feedback is invaluable to us

If you recently bought this book, we would love to hear from you! You can do this by writing a review on amazon (or the online store where you purchased this book) about your last purchase! As part of our continual service improvement process, we love to hear real client experiences and feedback.

How does it work?
To post a review on Amazon, just log in to your account and click on the Create Your Own Review button (under Customer Reviews) of the relevant product page. You can find examples of product reviews in Amazon. If you purchased from another online store, simply follow their procedures.

What happens when I submit my review?
Once you have submitted your review, send us an email at review@theartofservice.com with the link to your review so we can properly thank you for your feedback.

Purpose of this Self-Assessment

This Self-Assessment has been developed to improve understanding of the requirements and elements of Cloud Service Provider, based on best practices and standards in business process architecture, design and quality management.

It is designed to allow for a rapid Self-Assessment to determine how closely existing management practices and procedures correspond to the elements of the Self-Assessment.

The criteria of requirements and elements of Cloud Service Provider have been rephrased in the format of a Self-Assessment questionnaire, with a seven-criterion scoring system, as explained in this document.

In this format, even with limited background knowledge of Cloud

Service Provider, a manager can quickly review existing operations to determine how they measure up to the standards. This in turn can serve as the starting point of a 'gap analysis' to identify management tools or system elements that might usefully be implemented in the organization to help improve overall performance.

How to use the Self-Assessment

On the following pages are a series of questions to identify to what extent your Cloud Service Provider initiative is complete in comparison to the requirements set in standards.

To facilitate answering the questions, there is a space in front of each question to enter a score on a scale of '1' to '5'.

1 Strongly Disagree

2 Disagree

3 Neutral

4 Agree

5 Strongly Agree

Read the question and rate it with the following in front of mind:

'In my belief,
the answer to this question is clearly defined'.

There are two ways in which you can choose to interpret this statement;
   1.   how aware are you that the answer to the question is clearly defined
   2.   for more in-depth analysis you can choose to gather

evidence and confirm the answer to the question. This obviously will take more time, most Self-Assessment users opt for the first way to interpret the question and dig deeper later on based on the outcome of the overall Self-Assessment.

A score of '1' would mean that the answer is not clear at all, where a '5' would mean the answer is crystal clear and defined. Leave emtpy when the question is not applicable or you don't want to answer it, you can skip it without affecting your score. Write your score in the space provided.

After you have responded to all the appropriate statements in each section, compute your average score for that section, using the formula provided, and round to the nearest tenth. Then transfer to the corresponding spoke in the Cloud Service Provider Scorecard on the second next page of the Self-Assessment.

Your completed Cloud Service Provider Scorecard will give you a clear presentation of which Cloud Service Provider areas need attention.

Cloud Service Provider Scorecard Example

Example of how the finalized Scorecard can look like:

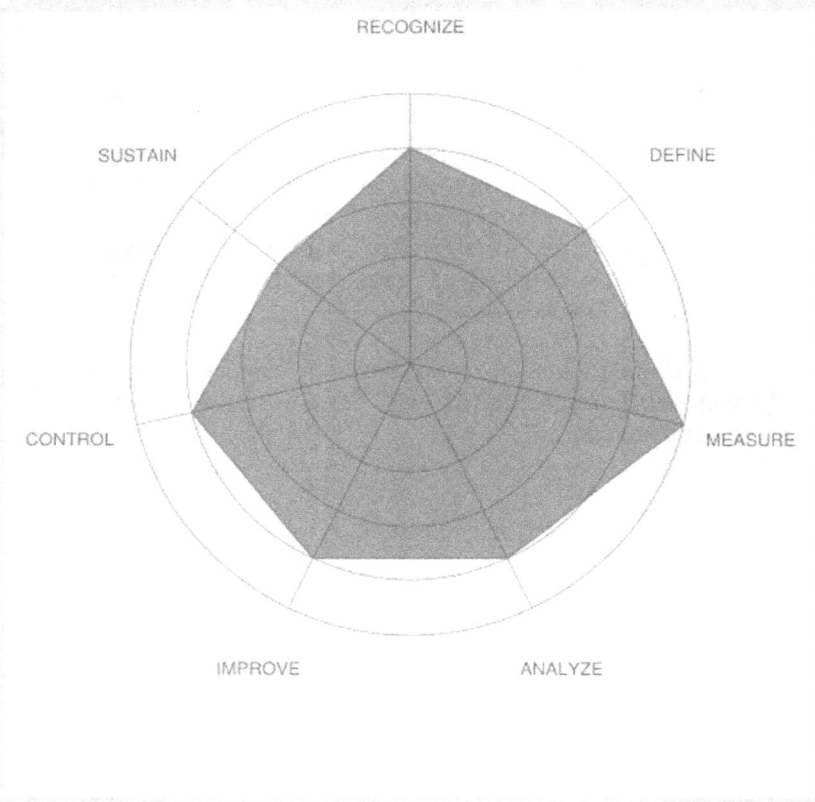

Cloud Service Provider Scorecard

Your Scores:

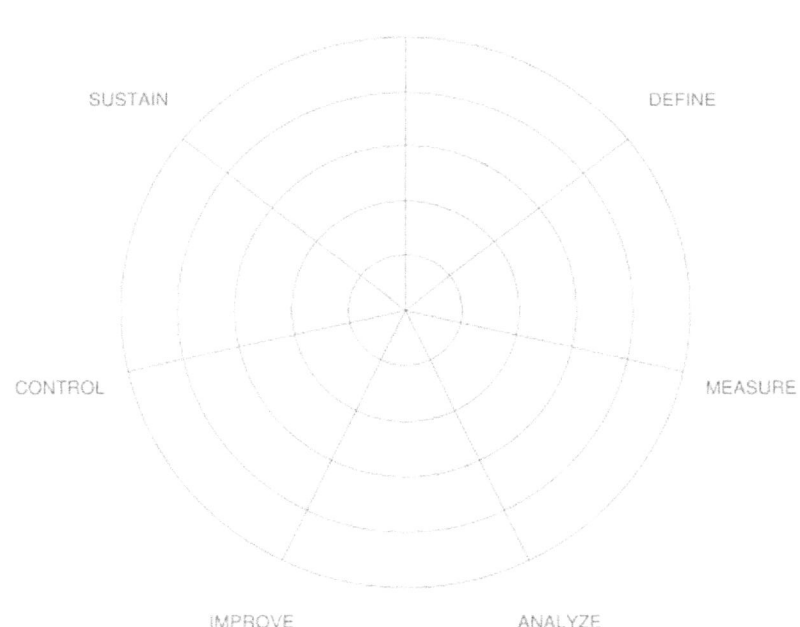

BEGINNING OF THE SELF-ASSESSMENT:

CRITERION #1: RECOGNIZE

INTENT: Be aware of the need for change. Recognize that there is an unfavorable variation, problem or symptom.

In my belief, the answer to this question is clearly defined:

5 Strongly Agree

4 Agree

3 Neutral

2 Disagree

1 Strongly Disagree

1. What are the stakeholder objectives to be achieved with cloud service provider?
<--- Score

2. Where do you need to exercise leadership?
<--- Score

3. Who should resolve the cloud service provider issues?

<--- Score

4. Who needs to know about cloud service provider?
<--- Score

5. Do you need to avoid or amend any cloud service provider activities?
<--- Score

6. What cloud service provider capabilities do you need?
<--- Score

7. What is the extent or complexity of the cloud service provider problem?
<--- Score

8. What training and capacity building actions are needed to implement proposed reforms?
<--- Score

9. How are training requirements identified?
<--- Score

10. How do you recognize an cloud service provider objection?
<--- Score

11. What extra resources will you need?
<--- Score

12. Are losses recognized in a timely manner?
<--- Score

13. What are your needs in relation to cloud service provider skills, labor, equipment, and markets?

<--- Score

14. What are the cloud service provider resources needed?
<--- Score

15. Are your goals realistic? Do you need to redefine your problem? Perhaps the problem has changed or maybe you have reached your goal and need to set a new one?
<--- Score

16. For your cloud service provider project, identify and describe the business environment, is there more than one layer to the business environment?
<--- Score

17. What resources or support might you need?
<--- Score

18. Who else hopes to benefit from it?
<--- Score

19. How much are sponsors, customers, partners, stakeholders involved in cloud service provider? In other words, what are the risks, if cloud service provider does not deliver successfully?
<--- Score

20. Why is this needed?
<--- Score

21. Are you dealing with any of the same issues today as yesterday? What can you do about this?
<--- Score

22. Think about the people you identified for your cloud service provider project and the project responsibilities you would assign to them, what kind of training do you think they would need to perform these responsibilities effectively?
<--- Score

23. Who are your key stakeholders who need to sign off?
<--- Score

24. What situation(s) led to this cloud service provider Self Assessment?
<--- Score

25. How do you assess your cloud service provider workforce capability and capacity needs, including skills, competencies, and staffing levels?
<--- Score

26. Do you need different information or graphics?
<--- Score

27. Consider your own cloud service provider project, what types of organizational problems do you think might be causing or affecting your problem, based on the work done so far?
<--- Score

28. Are problem definition and motivation clearly presented?
<--- Score

29. Can management personnel recognize the monetary benefit of cloud service provider?
<--- Score

30. Are employees recognized or rewarded for performance that demonstrates the highest levels of integrity?
<--- Score

31. What are the minority interests and what amount of minority interests can be recognized?
<--- Score

32. Why the need?
<--- Score

33. How do you take a forward-looking perspective in identifying cloud service provider research related to market response and models?
<--- Score

34. Will new equipment/products be required to facilitate cloud service provider delivery, for example is new software needed?
<--- Score

35. Where is training needed?
<--- Score

36. Are there recognized cloud service provider problems?
<--- Score

37. Whom do you really need or want to serve?
<--- Score

38. What is the recognized need?
<--- Score

39. What cloud service provider coordination do you need?
<--- Score

40. Which needs are not included or involved?
<--- Score

41. Is it needed?
<--- Score

42. What vendors make products that address the cloud service provider needs?
<--- Score

43. What are the clients issues and concerns?
<--- Score

44. What prevents you from making the changes you know will make you a more effective cloud service provider leader?
<--- Score

45. What is the problem and/or vulnerability?
<--- Score

46. Does cloud service provider create potential expectations in other areas that need to be recognized and considered?
<--- Score

47. Is the quality assurance team identified?
<--- Score

48. What information do users need?
<--- Score

49. How does it fit into your organizational needs and tasks?
<--- Score

50. Are controls defined to recognize and contain problems?
<--- Score

51. Are there any specific expectations or concerns about the cloud service provider team, cloud service provider itself?
<--- Score

52. As a sponsor, customer or management, how important is it to meet goals, objectives?
<--- Score

53. Are employees recognized for desired behaviors?
<--- Score

54. How can auditing be a preventative security measure?
<--- Score

55. Have you identified your cloud service provider key performance indicators?
<--- Score

56. Are there regulatory / compliance issues?
<--- Score

57. Is the need for organizational change recognized?
<--- Score

58. Which issues are too important to ignore?
<--- Score

59. Does the problem have ethical dimensions?
<--- Score

60. Will a response program recognize when a crisis occurs and provide some level of response?
<--- Score

61. What cloud service provider events should you attend?
<--- Score

62. What do employees need in the short term?
<--- Score

63. Do you know what you need to know about cloud service provider?
<--- Score

64. Who needs budgets?
<--- Score

65. To what extent would your organization benefit from being recognized as a award recipient?
<--- Score

66. What tools and technologies are needed for a custom cloud service provider project?
<--- Score

67. What problems are you facing and how do you consider cloud service provider will circumvent those obstacles?
<--- Score

68. What should be considered when identifying

available resources, constraints, and deadlines?
<--- Score

69. Looking at each person individually – does every one have the qualities which are needed to work in this group?
<--- Score

70. How are the cloud service provider's objectives aligned to the group's overall stakeholder strategy?
<--- Score

71. Do you recognize cloud service provider achievements?
<--- Score

72. What does cloud service provider success mean to the stakeholders?
<--- Score

73. Does your organization need more cloud service provider education?
<--- Score

74. What needs to be done?
<--- Score

75. What would happen if cloud service provider weren't done?
<--- Score

76. Did you miss any major cloud service provider issues?
<--- Score

77. What is the cloud service provider problem

definition? What do you need to resolve?

<--- Score

78. Will cloud service provider deliverables need to be tested and, if so, by whom?

<--- Score

79. What creative shifts do you need to take?

<--- Score

80. What cloud service provider problem should be solved?

<--- Score

81. What needs to stay?

<--- Score

82. Are there any revenue recognition issues?

<--- Score

83. Do you have/need 24-hour access to key personnel?

<--- Score

84. How do you identify the kinds of information that you will need?

<--- Score

85. Do you need to have an audit of every cloud service provider?

<--- Score

86. What are the expected benefits of cloud service provider to the stakeholder?

<--- Score

87. How are you going to measure success?
<--- Score

88. What do you need to start doing?
<--- Score

89. How do you recognize an objection?
<--- Score

90. What is the problem or issue?
<--- Score

91. Who defines the rules in relation to any given issue?
<--- Score

92. Are there cloud service provider problems defined?
<--- Score

93. When a cloud service provider manager recognizes a problem, what options are available?
<--- Score

94. Who needs what information?
<--- Score

Add up total points for this section:
_____ = Total points for this section

Divided by: _____ (number of statements answered) = _____ Average score for this section

Transfer your score to the cloud service provider Index at the beginning of the

Self-Assessment.

CRITERION #2: DEFINE:

INTENT: Formulate the stakeholder problem. Define the problem, needs and objectives.

In my belief, the answer to this question is clearly defined:

5 Strongly Agree

4 Agree

3 Neutral

2 Disagree

1 Strongly Disagree

1. Do you have organizational privacy requirements?
<--- Score

2. Can cloud service providers offer the flexibility to provide availability service levels in line with the customers requirements?
<--- Score

3. What are (control) requirements for cloud service

provider Information?
<--- Score

4. What cloud service provider services do you require?
<--- Score

5. Has your scope been defined?
<--- Score

6. Do you all define cloud service provider in the same way?
<--- Score

7. What baselines are required to be defined and managed?
<--- Score

8. How would you define the culture at your organization, how susceptible is it to cloud service provider changes?
<--- Score

9. The political context: who holds power?
<--- Score

10. What is a worst-case scenario for losses?
<--- Score

11. When are meeting minutes sent out? Who is on the distribution list?
<--- Score

12. How do you manage unclear cloud service provider requirements?
<--- Score

13. What critical content must be communicated –
who, what, when, where, and how?
<--- Score

14. Will a cloud service provider production readiness
review be required?
<--- Score

15. What is the scope of the cloud service provider
effort?
<--- Score

16. What sort of initial information to gather?
<--- Score

17. Is special cloud service provider user knowledge
required?
<--- Score

**18. Does the service agreement require that all
security terms must also pass down to any peer
service providers used by the provider?**
<--- Score

19. How will variation in the actual durations of each
activity be dealt with to ensure that the expected
cloud service provider results are met?
<--- Score

20. What information do you gather?
<--- Score

21. How do you gather the stories?
<--- Score

22. What customer feedback methods were used to solicit their input?
<--- Score

23. Has the improvement team collected the 'voice of the customer' (obtained feedback – qualitative and quantitative)?
<--- Score

24. What intelligence can you gather?
<--- Score

25. How do you keep key subject matter experts in the loop?
<--- Score

26. Are task requirements clearly defined?
<--- Score

27. Have the customer needs been translated into specific, measurable requirements? How?
<--- Score

28. What information should you gather?
<--- Score

29. What was the context?
<--- Score

30. Are audit criteria, scope, frequency and methods defined?
<--- Score

31. Is there a completed SIPOC representation, describing the Suppliers, Inputs, Process, Outputs, and Customers?

<--- Score

32. Is the improvement team aware of the different versions of a process: what they think it is vs. what it actually is vs. what it should be vs. what it could be?
<--- Score

33. Are customers identified and high impact areas defined?
<--- Score

34. Are the cloud service provider requirements testable?
<--- Score

35. What is the definition of success?
<--- Score

36. What is out of scope?
<--- Score

37. Is a fully trained team formed, supported, and committed to work on the cloud service provider improvements?
<--- Score

38. What is in scope?
<--- Score

39. Do you have a cloud service provider success story or case study ready to tell and share?
<--- Score

40. Is there any additional cloud service provider definition of success?
<--- Score

41. Is there a cloud service provider management charter, including stakeholder case, problem and goal statements, scope, milestones, roles and responsibilities, communication plan?
<--- Score

42. How do you gather requirements?
<--- Score

43. What is in the scope and what is not in scope?
<--- Score

44. Are the cloud service provider requirements complete?
<--- Score

45. Are required metrics defined, what are they?
<--- Score

46. Has anyone else (internal or external to the group) attempted to solve this problem or a similar one before? If so, what knowledge can be leveraged from these previous efforts?
<--- Score

47. Is it clearly defined in and to your organization what you do?
<--- Score

48. What are the dynamics of the communication plan?
<--- Score

49. How and when will the baselines be defined?
<--- Score

50. What are the boundaries of the scope? What is in bounds and what is not? What is the start point? What is the stop point?
<--- Score

51. What cloud service provider requirements should be gathered?
<--- Score

52. Are accountability and ownership for cloud service provider clearly defined?
<--- Score

53. What happens if cloud service provider's scope changes?
<--- Score

54. When is the estimated completion date?
<--- Score

55. What sources do you use to gather information for a cloud service provider study?
<--- Score

56. How would you define cloud service provider leadership?
<--- Score

57. Has a high-level 'as is' process map been completed, verified and validated?
<--- Score

58. Is scope creep really all bad news?
<--- Score

59. How does the cloud service provider manager ensure against scope creep?
<--- Score

60. Is cloud service provider currently on schedule according to the plan?
<--- Score

61. Has everyone on the team, including the team leaders, been properly trained?
<--- Score

62. Is the cloud service provider scope manageable?
<--- Score

63. What is the context?
<--- Score

64. Does the service agreement require that all security terms must also pass down to any peer cloud service providers used by the provider?
<--- Score

65. How was the 'as is' process map developed, reviewed, verified and validated?
<--- Score

66. Is data collected and displayed to better understand customer(s) critical needs and requirements.
<--- Score

67. Why are you doing cloud service provider and what is the scope?
<--- Score

68. Who is gathering information?
<--- Score

69. What scope do you want your strategy to cover?
<--- Score

70. How did the cloud service provider manager receive input to the development of a cloud service provider improvement plan and the estimated completion dates/times of each activity?
<--- Score

71. Are all requirements met?
<--- Score

72. Is there a completed, verified, and validated high-level 'as is' (not 'should be' or 'could be') stakeholder process map?
<--- Score

73. What defines best in class?
<--- Score

74. Has/have the customer(s) been identified?
<--- Score

75. What would be the goal or target for a cloud service provider's improvement team?
<--- Score

76. How do you gather cloud service provider requirements?
<--- Score

77. Will team members regularly document their cloud service provider work?

<--- Score

78. What system do you use for gathering cloud service provider information?
<--- Score

79. Will team members perform cloud service provider work when assigned and in a timely fashion?
<--- Score

80. Who is gathering cloud service provider information?
<--- Score

81. Does your cloud service provider meet your security requirements?
<--- Score

82. What is the scope of the cloud service provider work?
<--- Score

83. Is there a clear cloud service provider case definition?
<--- Score

84. Have all of the relationships been defined properly?
<--- Score

85. What scope to assess?
<--- Score

86. Is the team formed and are team leaders (Coaches and Management Leads) assigned?
<--- Score

87. How have you defined all cloud service provider requirements first?
<--- Score

88. How do you hand over cloud service provider context?
<--- Score

89. How will the cloud service provider team and the group measure complete success of cloud service provider?
<--- Score

90. Are team charters developed?
<--- Score

91. Is there regularly 100% attendance at the team meetings? If not, have appointed substitutes attended to preserve cross-functionality and full representation?
<--- Score

92. Is full participation by members in regularly held team meetings guaranteed?
<--- Score

93. Who are the cloud service provider improvement team members, including Management Leads and Coaches?
<--- Score

94. What gets examined?
<--- Score

95. What specifically is the problem? Where does it

occur? When does it occur? What is its extent?

<--- Score

96. Have all basic functions of cloud service provider been defined?

<--- Score

97. What constraints exist that might impact the team?

<--- Score

98. Has the cloud service provider work been fairly and/or equitably divided and delegated among team members who are qualified and capable to perform the work? Has everyone contributed?

<--- Score

99. Is the current 'as is' process being followed? If not, what are the discrepancies?

<--- Score

100. What are the cloud service provider tasks and definitions?

<--- Score

101. What key stakeholder process output measure(s) does cloud service provider leverage and how?

<--- Score

102. Has a project plan, Gantt chart, or similar been developed/completed?

<--- Score

103. Is the cloud service provider scope complete and appropriately sized?

<--- Score

104. What are the requirements for audit information?
<--- Score

105. What are the Roles and Responsibilities for each team member and its leadership? Where is this documented?
<--- Score

106. Is the team equipped with available and reliable resources?
<--- Score

107. Does the team have regular meetings?
<--- Score

108. Has a cloud service provider requirement not been met?
<--- Score

109. Are different versions of process maps needed to account for the different types of inputs?
<--- Score

110. Do the problem and goal statements meet the SMART criteria (specific, measurable, attainable, relevant, and time-bound)?
<--- Score

111. Are improvement team members fully trained on cloud service provider?
<--- Score

112. Is the team adequately staffed with the desired cross-functionality? If not, what additional resources are available to the team?

<--- Score

113. How is the team tracking and documenting its work?
<--- Score

114. How do you think the partners involved in cloud service provider would have defined success?
<--- Score

115. What are the tasks and definitions?
<--- Score

116. What is out-of-scope initially?
<--- Score

117. Is cloud service provider linked to key stakeholder goals and objectives?
<--- Score

118. If substitutes have been appointed, have they been briefed on the cloud service provider goals and received regular communications as to the progress to date?
<--- Score

119. Has your cloud service provider met your regulatory requirements?
<--- Score

120. Does the cloud service provider require third-party providers in order to deliver services?
<--- Score

121. Is the team sponsored by a champion or stakeholder leader?

<--- Score

122. What are the compelling stakeholder reasons for embarking on cloud service provider?
<--- Score

123. Has a team charter been developed and communicated?
<--- Score

124. What are the record-keeping requirements of cloud service provider activities?
<--- Score

125. What is the definition of cloud service provider excellence?
<--- Score

126. Are stakeholder processes mapped?
<--- Score

127. Have specific policy objectives been defined?
<--- Score

128. How do you manage scope?
<--- Score

129. When is/was the cloud service provider start date?
<--- Score

130. Has the direction changed at all during the course of cloud service provider? If so, when did it change and why?
<--- Score

131. Are customer(s) identified and segmented according to their different needs and requirements?
<--- Score

132. Who defines (or who defined) the rules and roles?
<--- Score

133. How often are the team meetings?
<--- Score

134. Are the slas from a cloud service provider sufficient to meet slas requirements for your customer?
<--- Score

135. Are approval levels defined for contracts and supplements to contracts?
<--- Score

136. Scope of sensitive information?
<--- Score

137. Is there a critical path to deliver cloud service provider results?
<--- Score

138. Are there different segments of customers?
<--- Score

139. What are the rough order estimates on cost savings/opportunities that cloud service provider brings?
<--- Score

140. How do you build the right business case?
<--- Score

141. Are there any constraints known that bear on the ability to perform cloud service provider work? How is the team addressing them?
<--- Score

Add up total points for this section:
_____ = Total points for this section

Divided by: _____ (number of statements answered) = _____
Average score for this section

Transfer your score to the cloud service provider Index at the beginning of the Self-Assessment.

CRITERION #3: MEASURE:

INTENT: Gather the correct data.
Measure the current performance and
evolution of the situation.

In my belief, the answer to this
question is clearly defined:

5 Strongly Agree

4 Agree

3 Neutral

2 Disagree

1 Strongly Disagree

1. What are the costs of delaying cloud service
provider action?
<--- Score

2. What are your key cloud service provider indicators
that you will measure, analyze and track?
<--- Score

3. How do you know that any cloud service provider

analysis is complete and comprehensive?
<--- Score

4. Are the units of measure consistent?
<--- Score

5. How will costs be allocated?
<--- Score

6. Where is it measured?
<--- Score

7. How does cost-to-serve analysis help?
<--- Score

8. What is measured? Why?
<--- Score

9. Do you aggressively reward and promote the people who have the biggest impact on creating excellent cloud service provider services/products?
<--- Score

10. Where can you go to verify the info?
<--- Score

11. How will success or failure be measured?
<--- Score

12. Who pays the cost?
<--- Score

13. Is the solution cost-effective?
<--- Score

14. What do people want to verify?

<--- Score

15. How are measurements made?
<--- Score

16. Who is involved in verifying compliance?
<--- Score

17. What is your cloud service provider quality cost segregation study?
<--- Score

18. What are your key cloud service provider organizational performance measures, including key short and longer-term financial measures?
<--- Score

19. What could cause delays in the schedule?
<--- Score

20. Can you do cloud service provider without complex (expensive) analysis?
<--- Score

21. What are the types and number of measures to use?
<--- Score

22. Are indirect costs charged to the cloud service provider program?
<--- Score

23. How large is the gap between current performance and the customer-specified (goal) performance?
<--- Score

24. What are your primary costs, revenues, assets?
<--- Score

25. What are the strategic priorities for this year?
<--- Score

26. What are the costs of reform?
<--- Score

27. Does cloud service provider systematically track and analyze outcomes for accountability and quality improvement?
<--- Score

28. How do you measure efficient delivery of cloud service provider services?
<--- Score

29. What has the team done to assure the stability and accuracy of the measurement process?
<--- Score

30. How do you identify and analyze stakeholders and their interests?
<--- Score

31. Are there competing cloud service provider priorities?
<--- Score

32. Are you taking your company in the direction of better and revenue or cheaper and cost?
<--- Score

33. What charts has the team used to display the

components of variation in the process?
<--- Score

34. Do you have a flow diagram of what happens?
<--- Score

35. What is your decision requirements diagram?
<--- Score

36. What is an unallowable cost?
<--- Score

37. How will measures be used to manage and adapt?
<--- Score

38. Which cloud service provider impacts are significant?
<--- Score

39. What causes innovation to fail or succeed in your organization?
<--- Score

40. How do you prevent mis-estimating cost?
<--- Score

41. Are process variation components displayed/ communicated using suitable charts, graphs, plots?
<--- Score

42. What drives O&M cost?
<--- Score

43. How can you manage cost down?
<--- Score

44. How do you verify the cloud service provider requirements quality?
<--- Score

45. How sensitive must the cloud service provider strategy be to cost?
<--- Score

46. What harm might be caused?
<--- Score

47. What causes investor action?
<--- Score

48. How will your organization measure success?
<--- Score

49. Do you have any cost cloud service provider limitation requirements?
<--- Score

50. Do you verify that corrective actions were taken?
<--- Score

51. When is Root Cause Analysis Required?
<--- Score

52. What does a Test Case verify?
<--- Score

53. Are the measurements objective?
<--- Score

54. Are cloud service provider vulnerabilities categorized and prioritized?
<--- Score

55. Have the concerns of stakeholders to help identify and define potential barriers been obtained and analyzed?
<--- Score

56. What would be a real cause for concern?
<--- Score

57. Which costs should be taken into account?
<--- Score

58. How can you measure cloud service provider in a systematic way?
<--- Score

59. What does verifying compliance entail?
<--- Score

60. Which measures and indicators matter?
<--- Score

61. How do you verify and develop ideas and innovations?
<--- Score

62. Do you effectively measure and reward individual and team performance?
<--- Score

63. How can you measure the performance?
<--- Score

64. How do you focus on what is right -not who is right?
<--- Score

65. How do you measure lifecycle phases?
<--- Score

66. Was a life-cycle cost analysis performed?
<--- Score

67. Do staff have the necessary skills to collect, analyze, and report data?
<--- Score

68. Is there a Performance Baseline?
<--- Score

69. When are costs are incurred?
<--- Score

70. Will cloud service provider have an impact on current business continuity, disaster recovery processes and/or infrastructure?
<--- Score

71. What are the cloud service provider investment costs?
<--- Score

72. What details are required of the cloud service provider cost structure?
<--- Score

73. Are there measurements based on task performance?
<--- Score

74. What particular quality tools did the team find helpful in establishing measurements?

<--- Score

75. Are you aware of what could cause a problem?
<--- Score

76. How do you measure success?
<--- Score

77. What are hidden cloud service provider quality costs?
<--- Score

78. What disadvantage does this cause for the user?
<--- Score

79. How can a cloud service provider test verify your ideas or assumptions?
<--- Score

80. What are the operational costs after cloud service provider deployment?
<--- Score

81. Is it possible to estimate the impact of unanticipated complexity such as wrong or failed assumptions, feedback, etcetera on proposed reforms?
<--- Score

82. What measurements are possible, practicable and meaningful?
<--- Score

83. How is the value delivered by cloud service provider being measured?
<--- Score

84. What relevant entities could be measured?
<--- Score

85. How frequently do you track cloud service provider measures?
<--- Score

86. Does the cloud service provider task fit the client's priorities?
<--- Score

87. How do you verify performance?
<--- Score

88. What are the costs?
<--- Score

89. Is a solid data collection plan established that includes measurement systems analysis?
<--- Score

90. Are high impact defects defined and identified in the stakeholder process?
<--- Score

91. Does your organization systematically track and analyze outcomes related for accountability and quality improvement?
<--- Score

92. What methods are feasible and acceptable to estimate the impact of reforms?
<--- Score

93. What are allowable costs?

<--- Score

94. Which stakeholder characteristics are analyzed?
<--- Score

95. How is progress measured?
<--- Score

96. How do you do risk analysis of rare, cascading, catastrophic events?
<--- Score

97. How do you verify your resources?
<--- Score

98. What tests verify requirements?
<--- Score

99. How will the cloud service provider data be analyzed?
<--- Score

100. How will you measure success?
<--- Score

101. Was a data collection plan established?
<--- Score

102. Is the cost worth the cloud service provider effort ?
<--- Score

103. What is the cause of any cloud service provider gaps?
<--- Score

104. Has a cost benefit analysis been performed?
<--- Score

105. What causes mismanagement?
<--- Score

106. What would it cost to replace your technology?
<--- Score

107. What is the cost of rework?
<--- Score

108. What key measures identified indicate the performance of the stakeholder process?
<--- Score

109. Is long term and short term variability accounted for?
<--- Score

110. Is data collection planned and executed?
<--- Score

111. What are the agreed upon definitions of the high impact areas, defect(s), unit(s), and opportunities that will figure into the process capability metrics?
<--- Score

112. What could cause you to change course?
<--- Score

113. Have you found any 'ground fruit' or 'low-hanging fruit' for immediate remedies to the gap in performance?
<--- Score

114. Who participated in the data collection for measurements?
<--- Score

115. Are there any easy-to-implement alternatives to cloud service provider? Sometimes other solutions are available that do not require the cost implications of a full-blown project?
<--- Score

116. Is data collected on key measures that were identified?
<--- Score

117. What is the total fixed cost?
<--- Score

118. Have you made assumptions about the shape of the future, particularly its impact on your customers and competitors?
<--- Score

119. What are the costs and benefits?
<--- Score

120. How do you verify the authenticity of the data and information used?
<--- Score

121. What are predictive cloud service provider analytics?
<--- Score

122. How will effects be measured?
<--- Score

123. How will you measure your cloud service provider effectiveness?
<--- Score

124. What causes extra work or rework?
<--- Score

125. What is your cost benefit analysis?
<--- Score

126. Was a business case (cost/benefit) developed?
<--- Score

127. How do you control the overall costs of your work processes?
<--- Score

128. Why a cloud service provider focus?
<--- Score

129. How are costs allocated?
<--- Score

130. Has a cost center been established?
<--- Score

131. What is the root cause(s) of the problem?
<--- Score

132. How do you aggregate measures across priorities?
<--- Score

133. Is Process Variation Displayed/Communicated?
<--- Score

134. Have design-to-cost goals been established?
<--- Score

135. What happens if cost savings do not materialize?
<--- Score

136. Did you tackle the cause or the symptom?
<--- Score

137. Are losses documented, analyzed, and remedial processes developed to prevent future losses?
<--- Score

138. Is there an opportunity to verify requirements?
<--- Score

139. At what cost?
<--- Score

140. Among the cloud service provider product and service cost to be estimated, which is considered hardest to estimate?
<--- Score

141. What measurements are being captured?
<--- Score

142. Are missed cloud service provider opportunities costing your organization money?
<--- Score

143. Have the types of risks that may impact cloud service provider been identified and analyzed?
<--- Score

144. How do you verify if cloud service provider is

built right?
<--- Score

145. Does cloud service provider analysis isolate the fundamental causes of problems?
<--- Score

146. Is the scope of cloud service provider cost analysis cost-effective?
<--- Score

147. How do you stay flexible and focused to recognize larger cloud service provider results?
<--- Score

148. How can you reduce the costs of obtaining inputs?
<--- Score

149. What evidence is there and what is measured?
<--- Score

150. How do your measurements capture actionable cloud service provider information for use in exceeding your customers expectations and securing your customers engagement?
<--- Score

151. What is the right balance of time and resources between investigation, analysis, and discussion and dissemination?
<--- Score

152. How frequently do you verify your cloud service provider strategy?
<--- Score

153. Are key measures identified and agreed upon?
<--- Score

154. What can be used to verify compliance?
<--- Score

155. What are you verifying?
<--- Score

156. What are the cloud service provider key cost drivers?
<--- Score

157. How do you quantify and qualify impacts?
<--- Score

158. Are you able to realize any cost savings?
<--- Score

159. How do you measure variability?
<--- Score

160. Have all non-recommended alternatives been analyzed in sufficient detail?
<--- Score

161. What are the uncertainties surrounding estimates of impact?
<--- Score

162. What does losing customers cost your organization?
<--- Score

163. When a disaster occurs, who gets priority?

<--- Score

164. The approach of traditional cloud service provider works for detail complexity but is focused on a systematic approach rather than an understanding of the nature of systems themselves, what approach will permit your organization to deal with the kind of unpredictable emergent behaviors that dynamic complexity can introduce?
<--- Score

165. Will it allow users to move their data or their applications between multiple cloud service providers at low cost and with minimal disruption?
<--- Score

166. Does a cloud service provider quantification method exist?
<--- Score

167. How do you verify and validate the cloud service provider data?
<--- Score

168. Is key measure data collection planned and executed, process variation displayed and communicated and performance baselined?
<--- Score

169. Are actual costs in line with budgeted costs?
<--- Score

170. How do you verify cloud service provider completeness and accuracy?
<--- Score

171. What does your operating model cost?
<--- Score

172. How much does it cost?
<--- Score

173. What are the key input variables? What are the key process variables? What are the key output variables?
<--- Score

174. Do the benefits outweigh the costs?
<--- Score

175. What data was collected (past, present, future/ongoing)?
<--- Score

176. Why do the measurements/indicators matter?
<--- Score

177. What potential environmental factors impact the cloud service provider effort?
<--- Score

Add up total points for this section:
_ _ _ _ _ = Total points for this section

Divided by: _ _ _ _ _ _ (number of statements answered) = _ _ _ _ _ _
Average score for this section

Transfer your score to the cloud service provider Index at the beginning of the Self-Assessment.

CRITERION #4: ANALYZE:

INTENT: Analyze causes, assumptions and hypotheses.

In my belief, the answer to this question is clearly defined:

5 Strongly Agree

4 Agree

3 Neutral

2 Disagree

1 Strongly Disagree

1. What is the cloud service provider Driver?
<--- Score

2. Were any designed experiments used to generate additional insight into the data analysis?
<--- Score

3. Are all staff in core cloud service provider subjects Highly Qualified?
<--- Score

4. Is the performance gap determined?
<--- Score

5. Do your employees have the opportunity to do what they do best everyday?
<--- Score

6. Who is responsible for data security in the cloud?
<--- Score

7. What internal processes need improvement?
<--- Score

8. How will the change process be managed?
<--- Score

9. Should you invest in industry-recognized qualifications?
<--- Score

10. What is the cost of poor quality as supported by the team's analysis?
<--- Score

11. What other jobs or tasks affect the performance of the steps in the cloud service provider process?
<--- Score

12. How is the data gathered?
<--- Score

13. What output to create?
<--- Score

14. Was a cause-and-effect diagram used to explore the different types of causes (or sources of variation)?
<--- Score

15. What are your cloud service provider processes?
<--- Score

16. How do you identify specific cloud service provider investment opportunities and emerging trends?
<--- Score

17. What controls do you have in place to protect data?
<--- Score

18. How is the way you as the leader think and process information affecting your organizational culture?
<--- Score

19. What qualifications are necessary?
<--- Score

20. What are your current levels and trends in key cloud service provider measures or indicators of product and process performance that are important to and directly serve your customers?
<--- Score

21. What methods do you use to gather cloud service provider data?
<--- Score

22. Which cloud service provider data should be retained?
<--- Score

23. Will it allow users to retrieve their data and their application artifacts and to have strong assurance that the cloud service provider will delete all copies and not retain any materials belonging to the cloud service customer after an agreed period?

<--- Score

24. Think about some of the processes you undertake within your organization, which do you own?

<--- Score

25. Are you missing cloud service provider opportunities?

<--- Score

26. What does the data say about the performance of the stakeholder process?

<--- Score

27. What qualifies as competition?

<--- Score

28. What types of data do your cloud service provider indicators require?

<--- Score

29. Is the gap/opportunity displayed and communicated in financial terms?

<--- Score

30. Does the cloud service provider have a documented exception process for allowing legitimate traffic that the IDS/IPS flags as an attack pattern?

<--- Score

31. Do you have the authority to produce the output?
<--- Score

32. Was a detailed process map created to amplify critical steps of the 'as is' stakeholder process?
<--- Score

33. How do you implement and manage your work processes to ensure that they meet design requirements?
<--- Score

34. What are your key performance measures or indicators and in-process measures for the control and improvement of your cloud service provider processes?
<--- Score

35. What did the team gain from developing a sub-process map?
<--- Score

36. Do several people in different organizational units assist with the cloud service provider process?
<--- Score

37. Do staff qualifications match your project?
<--- Score

38. How do you use cloud service provider data and information to support organizational decision making and innovation?
<--- Score

39. What other organizational variables, such as reward systems or communication systems, affect the performance of this cloud service provider process?
<--- Score

40. Where can you get qualified talent today?
<--- Score

41. Who qualifies to gain access to data?
<--- Score

42. What process should you select for improvement?
<--- Score

43. Where is the data coming from to measure compliance?
<--- Score

44. What kind of crime could a potential new hire have committed that would not only not disqualify him/her from being hired by your organization, but would actually indicate that he/she might be a particularly good fit?
<--- Score

45. How many input/output points does it require?
<--- Score

46. What will drive cloud service provider change?
<--- Score

47. Do your leaders quickly bounce back from setbacks?
<--- Score

48. What are evaluation criteria for the output?

<--- Score

49. Has data output been validated?
<--- Score

50. Is there a strict change management process?
<--- Score

51. An organizationally feasible system request is one that considers the mission, goals and objectives of the organization, key questions are: is the cloud service provider solution request practical and will it solve a problem or take advantage of an opportunity to achieve company goals?
<--- Score

52. Is there an established process for what is supposed to occur when ownership of an authorized service transfers from one Cloud Service Provider (CSP) to another?
<--- Score

53. Who is involved with workflow mapping?
<--- Score

54. How do mission and objectives affect the cloud service provider processes of your organization?
<--- Score

55. What are your current levels and trends in key measures or indicators of cloud service provider product and process performance that are important to and directly serve your customers? How do these results compare with the performance of your competitors and other organizations with similar offerings?

<--- Score

56. What data do you need to collect?
<--- Score

57. What were the financial benefits resulting from any 'ground fruit or low-hanging fruit' (quick fixes)?
<--- Score

58. Did any additional data need to be collected?
<--- Score

59. Has an output goal been set?
<--- Score

60. What is the oversight process?
<--- Score

61. What is the complexity of the output produced?
<--- Score

62. Were there any improvement opportunities identified from the process analysis?
<--- Score

63. Identify an operational issue in your organization, for example, could a particular task be done more quickly or more efficiently by cloud service provider?
<--- Score

64. Can the service be combined with another one to qualify for higher discounts from the cloud service provider?
<--- Score

65. What is the Value Stream Mapping?

<--- Score

66. What information qualified as important?
<--- Score

67. What do you need to qualify?
<--- Score

68. Did any value-added analysis or 'lean thinking' take place to identify some of the gaps shown on the 'as is' process map?
<--- Score

69. What are your best practices for minimizing cloud service provider project risk, while demonstrating incremental value and quick wins throughout the cloud service provider project lifecycle?
<--- Score

70. What is the output?
<--- Score

71. Is the cloud service provider process severely broken such that a re-design is necessary?
<--- Score

72. Do cloud service providers have particularly challenging obligations for customer data security?
<--- Score

73. How do you measure the operational performance of your key work systems and processes, including productivity, cycle time, and other appropriate measures of process effectiveness, efficiency, and innovation?

<--- Score

74. What quality tools were used to get through the analyze phase?
<--- Score

75. How are outputs preserved and protected?
<--- Score

76. Will administrators have access to the virtual data?
<--- Score

77. What is the risk that your data will be delivered to a domestic or foreign law enforcement organization by the cloud service provider in response to a legally binding request?
<--- Score

78. What cloud service provider data should be collected?
<--- Score

79. Do your contracts/agreements contain data security obligations?
<--- Score

80. What is your organizations process which leads to recognition of value generation?
<--- Score

81. What data is gathered?
<--- Score

82. Who gets your output?
<--- Score

83. How does the organization define, manage, and improve its cloud service provider processes?
<--- Score

84. How often will data be collected for measures?
<--- Score

85. Have the problem and goal statements been updated to reflect the additional knowledge gained from the analyze phase?
<--- Score

86. How is the cloud service provider Value Stream Mapping managed?
<--- Score

87. Is data and process analysis, root cause analysis and quantifying the gap/opportunity in place?
<--- Score

88. What training and qualifications will you need?
<--- Score

89. Are all team members qualified for all tasks?
<--- Score

90. Is there an established change management process?
<--- Score

91. How do your work systems and key work processes relate to and capitalize on your core competencies?
<--- Score

92. What are the disruptive cloud service provider technologies that enable your organization to radically change your business processes?
<--- Score

93. Have any additional benefits been identified that will result from closing all or most of the gaps?
<--- Score

94. Record-keeping requirements flow from the records needed as inputs, outputs, controls and for transformation of a cloud service provider process, are the records needed as inputs to the cloud service provider process available?
<--- Score

95. What tools were used to narrow the list of possible causes?
<--- Score

96. Is the required cloud service provider data gathered?
<--- Score

97. Where is cloud service provider data gathered?
<--- Score

98. How quickly can the cloud service provider respond to questions?
<--- Score

99. What process improvements will be needed?
<--- Score

100. What are the revised rough estimates of the financial savings/opportunity for cloud service

provider improvements?
<--- Score

101. What is your organizations system for selecting qualified vendors?
<--- Score

102. Do you understand your management processes today?
<--- Score

103. What conclusions were drawn from the team's data collection and analysis? How did the team reach these conclusions?
<--- Score

104. Can your cloud service provider restore your data?
<--- Score

105. Are gaps between current performance and the goal performance identified?
<--- Score

106. Think about the functions involved in your cloud service provider project, what processes flow from these functions?
<--- Score

107. What qualifications are needed?
<--- Score

108. How has the cloud service provider data been gathered?
<--- Score

109. How difficult is it to qualify what cloud service provider ROI is?
<--- Score

110. How will the cloud service provider data be captured?
<--- Score

111. How do you define collaboration and team output?
<--- Score

112. A compounding model resolution with available relevant data can often provide insight towards a solution methodology; which cloud service provider models, tools and techniques are necessary?
<--- Score

113. Is the suppliers process defined and controlled?
<--- Score

114. Were Pareto charts (or similar) used to portray the 'heavy hitters' (or key sources of variation)?
<--- Score

115. Does the cloud service provider support the necessary management processes?
<--- Score

116. What are your outputs?
<--- Score

117. What are the necessary qualifications?
<--- Score

118. How do you promote understanding that

opportunity for improvement is not criticism of the status quo, or the people who created the status quo?
<--- Score

119. What were the crucial 'moments of truth' on the process map?
<--- Score

120. Can you add value to the current cloud service provider decision-making process (largely qualitative) by incorporating uncertainty modeling (more quantitative)?
<--- Score

121. Is the final output clearly identified?
<--- Score

122. What resources go in to get the desired output?
<--- Score

123. How was the detailed process map generated, verified, and validated?
<--- Score

124. Who is involved in the management review process?
<--- Score

125. What tools were used to generate the list of possible causes?
<--- Score

126. Have you defined which data is gathered how?
<--- Score

Add up total points for this section:

_____ = Total points for this section

Divided by: _____ (number of
statements answered) = _____
Average score for this section

Transfer your score to the cloud service
provider Index at the beginning of the
Self-Assessment.

CRITERION #5: IMPROVE:

INTENT: Develop a practical solution. Innovate, establish and test the solution and to measure the results.

In my belief, the answer to this question is clearly defined:

5 Strongly Agree

4 Agree

3 Neutral

2 Disagree

1 Strongly Disagree

1. How will you recognize and celebrate results?
<--- Score

2. Is there a small-scale pilot for proposed improvement(s)? What conclusions were drawn from the outcomes of a pilot?
<--- Score

3. How will you know when its improved?

<--- Score

4. What resources are required for the improvement efforts?
<--- Score

5. How does the solution remove the key sources of issues discovered in the analyze phase?
<--- Score

6. How can you improve performance?
<--- Score

7. What needs improvement? Why?
<--- Score

8. Is there a cost/benefit analysis of optimal solution(s)?
<--- Score

9. Are improved process ('should be') maps modified based on pilot data and analysis?
<--- Score

10. Is the solution technically practical?
<--- Score

11. Which of the recognised risks out of all risks can be most likely transferred?
<--- Score

12. Is a contingency plan established?
<--- Score

13. What attendant changes will need to be made to ensure that the solution is successful?

<--- Score

14. Who do you report cloud service provider results to?
<--- Score

15. What strategies for cloud service provider improvement are successful?
<--- Score

16. Describe the design of the pilot and what tests were conducted, if any?
<--- Score

17. How scalable is your cloud service provider solution?
<--- Score

18. Can the solution be designed and implemented within an acceptable time period?
<--- Score

19. Who are the people involved in developing and implementing cloud service provider?
<--- Score

20. How does your organization evaluate strategic cloud service provider success?
<--- Score

21. How can you better manage risk?
<--- Score

22. What practices helps your organization to develop its capacity to recognize patterns?
<--- Score

23. Is the optimal solution selected based on testing and analysis?
<--- Score

24. What error proofing will be done to address some of the discrepancies observed in the 'as is' process?
<--- Score

25. How do you measure progress and evaluate training effectiveness?
<--- Score

26. How risky is your organization?
<--- Score

27. How do you measure improved cloud service provider service perception, and satisfaction?
<--- Score

28. Who controls the risk?
<--- Score

29. Do you combine technical expertise with business knowledge and cloud service provider Key topics include lifecycles, development approaches, requirements and how to make a business case?
<--- Score

30. What should a proof of concept or pilot accomplish?
<--- Score

31. What tools do you use once you have decided on a cloud service provider strategy and more importantly how do you choose?

<--- Score

32. What is the magnitude of the improvements?
<--- Score

33. If you could go back in time five years, what decision would you make differently? What is your best guess as to what decision you're making today you might regret five years from now?
<--- Score

34. How can skill-level changes improve cloud service provider?
<--- Score

35. How do you manage and improve your cloud service provider work systems to deliver customer value and achieve organizational success and sustainability?
<--- Score

36. How will you know that a change is an improvement?
<--- Score

37. Who will be responsible for documenting the cloud service provider requirements in detail?
<--- Score

38. Is the cloud service provider risk managed?
<--- Score

39. Are new and improved process ('should be') maps developed?
<--- Score

40. Who manages cloud service provider risk?
<--- Score

41. Is the cloud service provider documentation thorough?
<--- Score

42. Do those selected for the cloud service provider team have a good general understanding of what cloud service provider is all about?
<--- Score

43. How do you mitigate cloud service provider risk?
<--- Score

44. Are there any constraints (technical, political, cultural, or otherwise) that would inhibit certain solutions?
<--- Score

45. How will you know that you have improved?
<--- Score

46. Is supporting cloud service provider documentation required?
<--- Score

47. Have you identified breakpoints and/or risk tolerances that will trigger broad consideration of a potential need for intervention or modification of strategy?
<--- Score

48. How do you improve cloud service provider service perception, and satisfaction?
<--- Score

49. How do you measure risk?
<--- Score

50. Are decisions made in a timely manner?
<--- Score

51. Do vendor agreements bring new compliance risk ?
<--- Score

52. What are the implications of the one critical cloud service provider decision 10 minutes, 10 months, and 10 years from now?
<--- Score

53. What are the affordable cloud service provider risks?
<--- Score

54. Where do the cloud service provider decisions reside?
<--- Score

55. What do you want to improve?
<--- Score

56. How can the phases of cloud service provider development be identified?
<--- Score

57. Are possible solutions generated and tested?
<--- Score

58. Does a good decision guarantee a good outcome?
<--- Score

59. What tools were most useful during the improve phase?
<--- Score

60. For decision problems, how do you develop a decision statement?
<--- Score

61. How do you link measurement and risk?
<--- Score

62. What are the expected cloud service provider results?
<--- Score

63. How can you improve cloud service provider?
<--- Score

64. What is cloud service provider's impact on utilizing the best solution(s)?
<--- Score

65. How do you improve your likelihood of success ?
<--- Score

66. How will the team or the process owner(s) monitor the implementation plan to see that it is working as intended?
<--- Score

67. How do you decide how much to remunerate an employee?
<--- Score

68. How do you keep improving cloud service

provider?
<--- Score

69. How significant is the improvement in the eyes of the end user?
<--- Score

70. Is any cloud service provider documentation required?
<--- Score

71. How do you go about comparing cloud service provider approaches/solutions?
<--- Score

72. Is the measure of success for cloud service provider understandable to a variety of people?
<--- Score

73. How do you define the solutions' scope?
<--- Score

74. What communications are necessary to support the implementation of the solution?
<--- Score

75. What are the concrete cloud service provider results?
<--- Score

76. What tools were used to evaluate the potential solutions?
<--- Score

77. Is pilot data collected and analyzed?
<--- Score

78. What tools were used to tap into the creativity and encourage 'outside the box' thinking?
<--- Score

79. Have you achieved cloud service provider improvements?
<--- Score

80. How do you deal with cloud service provider risk?
<--- Score

81. Are events managed to resolution?
<--- Score

82. cloud service provider risk decisions: whose call Is It?
<--- Score

83. What does the 'should be' process map/design look like?
<--- Score

84. Does the goal represent a desired result that can be measured?
<--- Score

85. How will you measure the results?
<--- Score

86. Is there a high likelihood that any recommendations will achieve their intended results?
<--- Score

87. What area needs the greatest improvement?
<--- Score

88. Where do you need cloud service provider improvement?
<--- Score

89. How are cloud service provider risks managed?
<--- Score

90. What went well, what should change, what can improve?
<--- Score

91. Who should make the cloud service provider decisions?
<--- Score

92. How do you improve productivity?
<--- Score

93. What lessons, if any, from a pilot were incorporated into the design of the full-scale solution?
<--- Score

94. Do you need to do a usability evaluation?
<--- Score

95. Are risk triggers captured?
<--- Score

96. To what extent does management recognize cloud service provider as a tool to increase the results?
<--- Score

97. What criteria will you use to assess your cloud service provider risks?
<--- Score

98. Explorations of the frontiers of cloud service provider will help you build influence, improve cloud service provider, optimize decision making, and sustain change, what is your approach?
<--- Score

99. Who controls key decisions that will be made?
<--- Score

100. What risks do you need to manage?
<--- Score

101. Is the implementation plan designed?
<--- Score

102. What improvements have been achieved?
<--- Score

103. Are you assessing cloud service provider and risk?
<--- Score

104. Risk factors: what are the characteristics of cloud service provider that make it risky?
<--- Score

105. Who will be responsible for making the decisions to include or exclude requested changes once cloud service provider is underway?
<--- Score

106. At what point will vulnerability assessments be performed once cloud service provider is put into production (e.g., ongoing Risk Management after implementation)?

<--- Score

107. What can you do to improve?
<--- Score

108. Were any criteria developed to assist the team in testing and evaluating potential solutions?
<--- Score

109. What actually has to improve and by how much?
<--- Score

110. What were the underlying assumptions on the cost-benefit analysis?
<--- Score

111. Who makes the cloud service provider decisions in your organization?
<--- Score

112. How does the team improve its work?
<--- Score

113. Is a solution implementation plan established, including schedule/work breakdown structure, resources, risk management plan, cost/budget, and control plan?
<--- Score

114. How do the cloud service provider results compare with the performance of your competitors and other organizations with similar offerings?
<--- Score

115. How do you manage cloud service provider risk?
<--- Score

116. Was a cloud service provider charter developed?
<--- Score

117. Who will be using the results of the measurement activities?
<--- Score

118. What were the criteria for evaluating a cloud service provider pilot?
<--- Score

119. Are the best solutions selected?
<--- Score

120. What is the risk?
<--- Score

121. How will the group know that the solution worked?
<--- Score

122. Is the scope clearly documented?
<--- Score

123. What is the team's contingency plan for potential problems occurring in implementation?
<--- Score

124. What is the implementation plan?
<--- Score

125. Risk Identification: What are the possible risk events your organization faces in relation to cloud service provider?
<--- Score

126. How did the team generate the list of possible solutions?
<--- Score

127. Was a pilot designed for the proposed solution(s)?
<--- Score

128. Who are the key stakeholders for the cloud service provider evaluation?
<--- Score

Add up total points for this section:
_ _ _ _ _ = Total points for this section

Divided by: _ _ _ _ _ _ (number of statements answered) = _ _ _ _ _ _
Average score for this section

Transfer your score to the cloud service provider Index at the beginning of the Self-Assessment.

CRITERION #6: CONTROL:

INTENT: Implement the practical solution. Maintain the performance and correct possible complications.

In my belief, the answer to this question is clearly defined:

5 Strongly Agree

4 Agree

3 Neutral

2 Disagree

1 Strongly Disagree

1. Is there documentation that will support the successful operation of the improvement?
<--- Score

2. Question to cloud service provider: Does your platform offer finegrained access control to enable segregation of duties?
<--- Score

3. Against what alternative is success being measured?
<--- Score

4. How will input, process, and output variables be checked to detect for sub-optimal conditions?
<--- Score

5. Is there a cloud service provider Communication plan covering who needs to get what information when?
<--- Score

6. How will new or emerging customer needs/requirements be checked/communicated to orient the process toward meeting the new specifications and continually reducing variation?
<--- Score

7. Is there a transfer of ownership and knowledge to process owner and process team tasked with the responsibilities.
<--- Score

8. What are the critical parameters to watch?
<--- Score

9. How do you spread information?
<--- Score

10. Is there a recommended audit plan for routine surveillance inspections of cloud service provider's gains?
<--- Score

11. Does the cloud service provider performance

meet the customer's requirements?
<--- Score

12. What itil best practices, security and data protection standards and guidelines are in use by the cloud service provider?
<--- Score

13. Are new process steps, standards, and documentation ingrained into normal operations?
<--- Score

14. How quickly can a cloud service provider scale services and capability and is this quick enough for the requirements of the customer/consumer?
<--- Score

15. You may have created your quality measures at a time when you lacked resources, technology wasn't up to the required standard, or low service levels were the industry norm. Have those circumstances changed?
<--- Score

16. What cloud service provider standards are applicable?
<--- Score

17. What key inputs and outputs are being measured on an ongoing basis?
<--- Score

18. Are there documented procedures?
<--- Score

19. Is a response plan in place for when the input,

process, or output measures indicate an 'out-of-control' condition?
<--- Score

20. What is the control/monitoring plan?
<--- Score

21. How do senior leaders actions reflect a commitment to the organizations cloud service provider values?
<--- Score

22. Have new or revised work instructions resulted?
<--- Score

23. Do the cloud service provider decisions you make today help people and the planet tomorrow?
<--- Score

24. Has the cloud service provider value of standards been quantified?
<--- Score

25. What is the standard for acceptable cloud service provider performance?
<--- Score

26. What is the best design framework for cloud service provider organization now that, in a post industrial-age if the top-down, command and control model is no longer relevant?
<--- Score

27. How do your controls stack up?
<--- Score

28. Is there an action plan in case of emergencies?
<--- Score

29. Implementation Planning: is a pilot needed to test the changes before a full roll out occurs?
<--- Score

30. Can applications and services use standard communication protocols and front-end access methods are supported by the client and the cloud service provider?
<--- Score

31. Can you adapt and adjust to changing cloud service provider situations?
<--- Score

32. Is there a control plan in place for sustaining improvements (short and long-term)?
<--- Score

33. What is the recommended frequency of auditing?
<--- Score

34. How will the process owner verify improvement in present and future sigma levels, process capabilities?
<--- Score

35. Will the team be available to assist members in planning investigations?
<--- Score

36. Has the improved process and its steps been standardized?
<--- Score

37. What are the performance and scale of the cloud service provider tools?

<--- Score

38. What are customers monitoring?

<--- Score

39. Can the cloud service provider demonstrate appropriate security controls applied to physical infrastructure and facilities?

<--- Score

40. What other areas of the group might benefit from the cloud service provider team's improvements, knowledge, and learning?

<--- Score

41. How likely is the current cloud service provider plan to come in on schedule or on budget?

<--- Score

42. Who controls critical resources?

<--- Score

43. How will the process owner and team be able to hold the gains?

<--- Score

44. Does the cloud service provider have necessary security controls on human resources?

<--- Score

45. Are documented procedures clear and easy to follow for the operators?

<--- Score

46. What is your theory of human motivation, and how does your compensation plan fit with that view?
<--- Score

47. Does a troubleshooting guide exist or is it needed?
<--- Score

48. What quality tools were useful in the control phase?
<--- Score

49. What are you attempting to measure/monitor?
<--- Score

50. How do you select, collect, align, and integrate cloud service provider data and information for tracking daily operations and overall organizational performance, including progress relative to strategic objectives and action plans?
<--- Score

51. What should you measure to verify efficiency gains?
<--- Score

52. Does job training on the documented procedures need to be part of the process team's education and training?
<--- Score

53. What do you measure to verify effectiveness gains?
<--- Score

54. How widespread is its use?
<--- Score

55. Where do ideas that reach policy makers and planners as proposals for cloud service provider strengthening and reform actually originate?
<--- Score

56. Who has control over resources?
<--- Score

57. Who will be in control?
<--- Score

58. How is change control managed?
<--- Score

59. Is a response plan established and deployed?
<--- Score

60. Does the response plan contain a definite closed loop continual improvement scheme (e.g., plan-do-check-act)?
<--- Score

61. Is the cloud service provider test/monitoring cost justified?
<--- Score

62. How do you monitor usage and cost?
<--- Score

63. How do you encourage people to take control and responsibility?
<--- Score

64. Are pertinent alerts monitored, analyzed and distributed to appropriate personnel?

<--- Score

65. Act/Adjust: What Do you Need to Do Differently?
<--- Score

66. How is cloud service provider project cost planned, managed, monitored?
<--- Score

67. Is new knowledge gained imbedded in the response plan?
<--- Score

68. How will report readings be checked to effectively monitor performance?
<--- Score

69. Are the planned controls working?
<--- Score

70. Can support from partners be adjusted?
<--- Score

71. Is there a documented and implemented monitoring plan?
<--- Score

72. What is your plan to assess your security risks?
<--- Score

73. Are operating procedures consistent?
<--- Score

74. Is reporting being used or needed?
<--- Score

75. Does cloud service provider appropriately measure and monitor risk?
<--- Score

76. How do you plan on providing proper recognition and disclosure of supporting companies?
<--- Score

77. Who is going to spread your message?
<--- Score

78. What other systems, operations, processes, and infrastructures (hiring practices, staffing, training, incentives/rewards, metrics/dashboards/scorecards, etc.) need updates, additions, changes, or deletions in order to facilitate knowledge transfer and improvements?
<--- Score

79. Will any special training be provided for results interpretation?
<--- Score

80. Can the cloud service provider make available an end-to-end continuity plan?
<--- Score

81. How will you measure your QA plan's effectiveness?
<--- Score

82. How do you plan for the cost of succession?
<--- Score

83. What are the known security controls?
<--- Score

84. Do you monitor the cloud service provider decisions made and fine tune them as they evolve?
<--- Score

85. Who is the cloud service provider process owner?
<--- Score

86. How will the day-to-day responsibilities for monitoring and continual improvement be transferred from the improvement team to the process owner?
<--- Score

87. What can you control?
<--- Score

88. Are the cloud service provider standards challenging?
<--- Score

89. What are your results for key measures or indicators of the accomplishment of your cloud service provider strategy and action plans, including building and strengthening core competencies?
<--- Score

90. How might the group capture best practices and lessons learned so as to leverage improvements?
<--- Score

91. Is there a standardized process?
<--- Score

92. Question to cloud service provider: What auditing logs, reports, alerts and notifications do

you provide in order to monitor user access both for your needs and for the needs of your auditor?
<--- Score

93. How should a cloud service provider (CSP) address platform scope within the System Security Plan (SSP)?
<--- Score

94. Is knowledge gained on process shared and institutionalized?
<--- Score

95. What adjustments to the strategies are needed?
<--- Score

96. What should the next improvement project be that is related to cloud service provider?
<--- Score

97. Does the cloud service provider have necessary security controls?
<--- Score

98. What do your reports reflect?
<--- Score

99. Are controls in place and consistently applied?
<--- Score

100. How do you establish and deploy modified action plans if circumstances require a shift in plans and rapid execution of new plans?
<--- Score

101. Are suggested corrective/restorative actions

indicated on the response plan for known causes to problems that might surface?
<--- Score

102. Who sets the cloud service provider standards?
<--- Score

103. How do controls support value?
<--- Score

Add up total points for this section:
_ _ _ _ _ = Total points for this section

Divided by: _ _ _ _ _ _ (number of statements answered) = _ _ _ _ _ _
Average score for this section

Transfer your score to the cloud service provider Index at the beginning of the Self-Assessment.

CRITERION #7: SUSTAIN:

INTENT: Retain the benefits.

In my belief, the answer to this
question is clearly defined:

5 Strongly Agree

4 Agree

3 Neutral

2 Disagree

1 Strongly Disagree

1. Political -is anyone trying to undermine this
project?
<--- Score

**2. How easy is it to migrate to another cloud
service provider?**
<--- Score

3. Are there any activities that you can take off your to
do list?
<--- Score

4. What is your formula for success in cloud service provider ?
<--- Score

5. Is your strategy driving your strategy? Or is the way in which you allocate resources driving your strategy?
<--- Score

6. How can you become more high-tech but still be high touch?
<--- Score

7. What you are going to do to affect the numbers?
<--- Score

8. Which models, tools and techniques are necessary?
<--- Score

9. Do you have the right people on the bus?
<--- Score

10. What new services of functionality will be implemented next with cloud service provider ?
<--- Score

11. What are the business goals cloud service provider is aiming to achieve?
<--- Score

12. Are your responses positive or negative?
<--- Score

13. How do you engage the workforce, in addition to satisfying them?
<--- Score

14. How do you lead with cloud service provider in mind?
<--- Score

15. What stupid rule would you most like to kill?
<--- Score

16. Is your basic point _____ or _____?
<--- Score

17. Are all key stakeholders present at all Structured Walkthroughs?
<--- Score

18. Why should people listen to you?
<--- Score

19. What may be the consequences for the performance of an organization if all stakeholders are not consulted regarding cloud service provider?
<--- Score

20. Question to cloud service provider: Do you offer single sign-on for access across multiple applications you offer, or trusted federated single sign-on across applications with other vendors?
<--- Score

21. How do you deal with cloud service provider changes?
<--- Score

22. What are specific cloud service provider rules to follow?
<--- Score

23. Do you think you know, or do you know you know ?

<--- Score

24. What happens when a new employee joins the organization?

<--- Score

25. What is the craziest thing you can do?

<--- Score

26. Which cloud service providers does your organization have a preference for?

<--- Score

27. What could happen if you do not do it?

<--- Score

28. Is the impact that cloud service provider has shown?

<--- Score

29. Why is it important to have senior management support for a cloud service provider project?

<--- Score

30. Is a cloud service provider breakthrough on the horizon?

<--- Score

31. Question to cloud service provider: What capability do you provide to facilitate privileged access reviews?

<--- Score

32. To whom do you add value?
<--- Score

33. Why is cloud service provider important for you now?
<--- Score

34. What was the last experiment you ran?
<--- Score

35. Are you maintaining a past–present–future perspective throughout the cloud service provider discussion?
<--- Score

36. Can you do all this work?
<--- Score

37. What knowledge, skills and characteristics mark a good cloud service provider project manager?
<--- Score

38. How will you motivate the stakeholders with the least vested interest?
<--- Score

39. If there were zero limitations, what would you do differently?
<--- Score

40. What are the key enablers to make this cloud service provider move?
<--- Score

41. If your company went out of business tomorrow, would anyone who doesn't get a paycheck here care?

<--- Score

42. How is implementation research currently incorporated into each of your goals?
<--- Score

43. How do you go about securing cloud service provider?
<--- Score

44. What did you miss in the interview for the worst hire you ever made?
<--- Score

45. Is cloud service provider realistic, or are you setting yourself up for failure?
<--- Score

46. How do you govern and fulfill your societal responsibilities?
<--- Score

47. How do you set cloud service provider stretch targets and how do you get people to not only participate in setting these stretch targets but also that they strive to achieve these?
<--- Score

48. How does cloud service provider integrate with other stakeholder initiatives?
<--- Score

49. What happens at your organization when people fail?
<--- Score

50. Who, on the executive team or the board, has spoken to a customer recently?
<--- Score

51. How will you insure seamless interoperability of cloud service provider moving forward?
<--- Score

52. Is the cloud service providers service desk local, onshore or offshore?
<--- Score

53. Were lessons learned captured and communicated?
<--- Score

54. Is maximizing cloud service provider protection the same as minimizing cloud service provider loss?
<--- Score

55. Who are the key stakeholders?
<--- Score

56. Did your employees make progress today?
<--- Score

57. What is the big cloud service provider idea?
<--- Score

58. Why should you adopt a cloud service provider framework?
<--- Score

59. How do you create buy-in?
<--- Score

60. Operational - will it work?
<--- Score

61. What type of auditing and logging capabilities are in place and how can they be accessed by the healthcare organization of the cloud service provider?
<--- Score

62. What current systems have to be understood and/ or changed?
<--- Score

63. Who will be responsible for deciding whether cloud service provider goes ahead or not after the initial investigations?
<--- Score

64. Who else should you help?
<--- Score

65. Are the criteria for selecting recommendations stated?
<--- Score

66. What is your BATNA (best alternative to a negotiated agreement)?
<--- Score

67. Who are four people whose careers you have enhanced?
<--- Score

68. What are the short and long-term cloud service provider goals?
<--- Score

69. How will you ensure you get what you expected?
<--- Score

70. Is there any existing cloud service provider governance structure?
<--- Score

71. How do you proactively clarify deliverables and cloud service provider quality expectations?
<--- Score

72. Are there too many tools or cloud service providers?
<--- Score

73. What is the range of capabilities?
<--- Score

74. How do you assess the cloud service provider pitfalls that are inherent in implementing it?
<--- Score

75. What are the top 3 things at the forefront of your cloud service provider agendas for the next 3 years?
<--- Score

76. What is your cloud service provider strategy?
<--- Score

77. Question to cloud service provider: Can you integrate your current IdAM system with your cloud services?
<--- Score

78. Question to cloud service provider: Does

strong authentication apply to both provider administrative roles and customer access?
<--- Score

79. Who will manage the integration of tools?
<--- Score

80. Question to cloud service provider: Does your platform offer delegated administration for your organization to administer users?
<--- Score

81. Who is the main stakeholder, with ultimate responsibility for driving cloud service provider forward?
<--- Score

82. How do your IT sourcing teams implement best practices into both traditional and cloud service provider environments?
<--- Score

83. Will there be any necessary staff changes (redundancies or new hires)?
<--- Score

84. What counts that you are not counting?
<--- Score

85. Will it be accepted by users?
<--- Score

86. What is the funding source for this project?
<--- Score

87. What are your personal philosophies regarding

cloud service provider and how do they influence your work?
<--- Score

88. Who do you want your customers to become?
<--- Score

89. Are assumptions made in cloud service provider stated explicitly?
<--- Score

90. Have benefits been optimized with all key stakeholders?
<--- Score

91. In retrospect, of the projects that you pulled the plug on, what percent do you wish had been allowed to keep going, and what percent do you wish had ended earlier?
<--- Score

92. If you do not follow, then how to lead?
<--- Score

93. Who have you, as a company, historically been when you've been at your best?
<--- Score

94. How do you foster innovation?
<--- Score

95. Are new benefits received and understood?
<--- Score

96. What are the gaps in your knowledge and experience?

<--- Score

97. Whose voice (department, ethnic group, women, older workers, etc) might you have missed hearing from in your company, and how might you amplify this voice to create positive momentum for your business?
<--- Score

98. What are the roles and responsibilities of the third party assessment organization (3PAO) and the cloud service provider (CSP) during the assessment?
<--- Score

99. How do you foster the skills, knowledge, talents, attributes, and characteristics you want to have?
<--- Score

100. Will the cloud service provider allow the CSA and FBI to conduct compliance and security audits?
<--- Score

101. What projects are going on in the organization today, and what resources are those projects using from the resource pools?
<--- Score

102. How do you determine the key elements that affect cloud service provider workforce satisfaction, how are these elements determined for different workforce groups and segments?
<--- Score

103. Which functions and people interact with the

supplier and or customer?
<--- Score

104. Do you feel that more should be done in the cloud service provider area?
<--- Score

105. Does the cloud service provider have sufficient back-to-back supporting contracts with the third party providers to ensure service provision to the customer?
<--- Score

106. What is the source of the strategies for cloud service provider strengthening and reform?
<--- Score

107. Is a cloud service provider team work effort in place?
<--- Score

108. What one word do you want to own in the minds of your customers, employees, and partners?
<--- Score

109. Who is responsible for errors?
<--- Score

110. Instead of going to current contacts for new ideas, what if you reconnected with dormant contacts--the people you used to know? If you were going reactivate a dormant tie, who would it be?
<--- Score

111. What cloud service provider skills are most important?

<--- Score

112. What is your question? Why?
<--- Score

113. Marketing budgets are tighter, consumers are more skeptical, and social media has changed forever the way we talk about cloud service provider, how do you gain traction?
<--- Score

114. Are you satisfied with your current role? If not, what is missing from it?
<--- Score

115. Do you have the right capabilities and capacities?
<--- Score

116. What is the purpose of cloud service provider in relation to the mission?
<--- Score

117. What are you trying to prove to yourself, and how might it be hijacking your life and business success?
<--- Score

118. How much does cloud service provider help?
<--- Score

119. What is the recommended frequency of auditing?
<--- Score

120. What unique value proposition (UVP) do you offer?
<--- Score

121. If your customer were your grandmother, would you tell her to buy what you're selling?
<--- Score

122. Who is responsible for cloud service provider?
<--- Score

123. What are internal and external cloud service provider relations?
<--- Score

124. Is the cloud service provider organization completing tasks effectively and efficiently?
<--- Score

125. Who are your customers?
<--- Score

126. Question to cloud service provider: If you cannot use your current IdAM system, what tools do you provide for onboarding and offboarding users?
<--- Score

127. How likely is it that a customer would recommend your company to a friend or colleague?
<--- Score

128. How do you provide a safe environment -physically and emotionally?
<--- Score

129. Have new benefits been realized?
<--- Score

130. How do you manage cloud service provider

Knowledge Management (KM)?
<--- Score

131. If you had to rebuild your organization without any traditional competitive advantages (i.e., no killer technology, promising research, innovative product/ service delivery model, etcetera), how would your people have to approach their work and collaborate together in order to create the necessary conditions for success?
<--- Score

132. How will you know that the cloud service provider project has been successful?
<--- Score

133. How do you ensure that implementations of cloud service provider products are done in a way that ensures safety?
<--- Score

134. What are the long-term cloud service provider goals?
<--- Score

135. What are the cloud service providers incident response procedures?
<--- Score

136. What are the rules and assumptions your industry operates under? What if the opposite were true?
<--- Score

137. What potential megatrends could make your business model obsolete?
<--- Score

138. Is cloud service provider dependent on the successful delivery of a current project?
<--- Score

139. How is the entire system protected from Internet threats?
<--- Score

140. Is there any reason to believe the opposite of my current belief?
<--- Score

141. Why not do cloud service provider?
<--- Score

142. If you had to leave your organization for a year and the only communication you could have with employees/colleagues was a single paragraph, what would you write?
<--- Score

143. How do you track customer value, profitability or financial return, organizational success, and sustainability?
<--- Score

144. At what moment would you think; Will I get fired?
<--- Score

145. Question to cloud service provider: Does your platform support the notion of Service ID and use of API Keys?
<--- Score

146. What is the overall talent health of your

organization as a whole at senior levels, and for each organization reporting to a member of the Senior Leadership Team?
<--- Score

147. Are you using a design thinking approach and integrating Innovation, cloud service provider Experience, and Brand Value?
<--- Score

148. Is it economical; do you have the time and money?
<--- Score

149. Can you break it down?
<--- Score

150. Are the assumptions believable and achievable?
<--- Score

151. What have been your experiences in defining long range cloud service provider goals?
<--- Score

152. What are the challenges?
<--- Score

153. In the past year, what have you done (or could you have done) to increase the accurate perception of your company/brand as ethical and honest?
<--- Score

154. Are you paying enough attention to the partners your company depends on to succeed?
<--- Score

155. What is a major difference between a true cloud service provider (CSP) and a managed service provider (MSP)?

<--- Score

156. What security arrangements do you have in place with cloud service providers you rely on to deliver your service?

<--- Score

157. What is the kind of project structure that would be appropriate for your cloud service provider project, should it be formal and complex, or can it be less formal and relatively simple?

<--- Score

158. What criteria are relevant for your organization when migrating to a cloud service provider?

<--- Score

159. Are you changing as fast as the world around you?

<--- Score

160. What is a feasible sequencing of reform initiatives over time?

<--- Score

161. Are you making progress, and are you making progress as cloud service provider leaders?

<--- Score

162. Who will provide the final approval of cloud service provider deliverables?

<--- Score

163. What would have to be true for the option on the table to be the best possible choice?
<--- Score

164. Question to cloud service provider: What forms of strong authentication does your platform support?
<--- Score

165. What is good cloud governance, and how did you achieve it?
<--- Score

166. Would you rather sell to knowledgeable and informed customers or to uninformed customers?
<--- Score

167. What is an unauthorized commitment?
<--- Score

168. Do cloud service provider rules make a reasonable demand on a users capabilities?
<--- Score

169. Who is responsible for recovery, you or the cloud service provider?
<--- Score

170. In a project to restructure cloud service provider outcomes, which stakeholders would you involve?
<--- Score

171. What is the estimated value of the project?
<--- Score

172. Do you see more potential in people than they do in themselves?
<--- Score

173. How do you keep the momentum going?
<--- Score

174. What are your most important goals for the strategic cloud service provider objectives?
<--- Score

175. How important is cloud service provider to the user organizations mission?
<--- Score

176. What threat is cloud service provider addressing?
<--- Score

177. What are strategies for increasing support and reducing opposition?
<--- Score

178. What are the success criteria that will indicate that cloud service provider objectives have been met and the benefits delivered?
<--- Score

179. What is something you believe that nearly no one agrees with you on?
<--- Score

180. How do you keep records, of what?
<--- Score

181. How can you become the company that would put you out of business?

<--- Score

182. How do you cross-sell and up-sell your cloud service provider success?
<--- Score

183. Who is on the team?
<--- Score

184. What are the essentials of internal cloud service provider management?
<--- Score

185. How do you maintain cloud service provider's Integrity?
<--- Score

186. How much contingency will be available in the budget?
<--- Score

187. What role does communication play in the success or failure of a cloud service provider project?
<--- Score

188. Who uses your product in ways you never expected?
<--- Score

189. How do you stay inspired?
<--- Score

190. How long will it take to change?
<--- Score

191. Who is responsible for ensuring appropriate

resources (time, people and money) are allocated to cloud service provider?

<--- Score

192. How do you accomplish your long range cloud service provider goals?

<--- Score

193. Which individuals, teams or departments will be involved in cloud service provider?

<--- Score

194. When information truly is ubiquitous, when reach and connectivity are completely global, when computing resources are infinite, and when a whole new set of impossibilities are not only possible, but happening, what will that do to your business?

<--- Score

195. What does your signature ensure?

<--- Score

196. Do you know who is a friend or a foe?

<--- Score

197. What relationships among cloud service provider trends do you perceive?

<--- Score

198. Do you have an implicit bias for capital investments over people investments?

<--- Score

199. What should you stop doing?

<--- Score

200. Why do and why don't your customers like your organization?

<--- Score

201. What should customers be looking for and expect from a good cloud service provider?

<--- Score

202. Are you relevant? Will you be relevant five years from now? Ten?

<--- Score

203. How do you transition from the baseline to the target?

<--- Score

204. Whom among your colleagues do you trust, and for what?

<--- Score

205. What management system can you use to leverage the cloud service provider experience, ideas, and concerns of the people closest to the work to be done?

<--- Score

206. What trouble can you get into?

<--- Score

207. What happens if you do not have enough funding?

<--- Score

208. How do you listen to customers to obtain actionable information?

<--- Score

209. What questions should be asked of a cloud service provider?

<--- Score

210. How can you incorporate support to ensure safe and effective use of cloud service provider into the services that you provide?

<--- Score

211. What are you challenging?

<--- Score

212. Which cloud service provider goals are the most important?

<--- Score

213. Is there a work around that you can use?

<--- Score

214. Do you know what you are doing? And who do you call if you don't?

<--- Score

215. What have you done to protect your business from competitive encroachment?

<--- Score

216. Is the cloud service provider financially stable?

<--- Score

217. How can you best use all of your knowledge repositories to enhance learning and sharing?

<--- Score

218. Who will determine interim and final deadlines?
<--- Score

219. What do we do when new problems arise?
<--- Score

220. What are the potential basics of cloud service provider fraud?
<--- Score

221. If you got fired and a new hire took your place, what would she do different?
<--- Score

222. If you find that you havent accomplished one of the goals for one of the steps of the cloud service provider strategy, what will you do to fix it?
<--- Score

223. What are the usability implications of cloud service provider actions?
<--- Score

224. What is it like to work for you?
<--- Score

225. Do you have past cloud service provider successes?
<--- Score

226. If you weren't already in this business, would you enter it today? And if not, what are you going to do about it?
<--- Score

227. What is effective cloud service provider?

<--- Score

228. Ask yourself: how would you do this work if you only had one staff member to do it?
<--- Score

Add up total points for this section:
_ _ _ _ _ = Total points for this section

Divided by: _ _ _ _ _ _ (number of statements answered) = _ _ _ _ _ _
Average score for this section

Transfer your score to the cloud service provider Index at the beginning of the Self-Assessment.

Cloud Service Provider and Managing Projects, Criteria for Project Managers:

1.0 Initiating Process Group: Cloud Service Provider

1. What were the challenges that you encountered during the execution of a previous Cloud Service Provider project that you would not want to repeat?

2. Who is funding the Cloud Service Provider project?

3. Do you know if the Cloud Service Provider project requires outside equipment or vendor resources?

4. Have the stakeholders identified all individual requirements pertaining to business process?

5. What technical work to do in each phase?

6. Who is involved in each phase?

7. For technology Cloud Service Provider projects only: Are all production support stakeholders (Business unit, technical support, & user) prepared for implementation with appropriate contingency plans?

8. What are the constraints?

9. At which cmmi level are software processes documented, standardized, and integrated into a standard to-be practiced process for your organization?

10. What is the stake of others in your Cloud Service Provider project?

11. What business situation is being addressed?

12. Based on your Cloud Service Provider project communication management plan, what worked well?

13. What will be the pressing issues of tomorrow?

14. How well did you do?

15. Do you know the Cloud Service Provider projects goal, purpose and objectives?

16. The Cloud Service Provider project managers have maximum authority in which type of organization?

17. Professionals want to know what is expected from them what are the deliverables?

18. Which six sigma dmaic phase focuses on why and how defects and errors occur?

19. What are the pressing issues of the hour?

20. What are the tools and techniques to be used in each phase?

1.1 Project Charter: Cloud Service Provider

21. How will you know that a change is an improvement?

22. Why the improvements?

23. Why is it important?

24. Run it as as a startup?

25. Major high-level milestone targets: what events measure progress?

26. Is it an improvement over existing products?

27. What goes into your Cloud Service Provider project Charter?

28. Are there special technology requirements?

29. Are you building in-house ?

30. Pop quiz – which are the same inputs as in the Cloud Service Provider project charter?

31. What changes can you make to improve?

32. Must Have?

33. Assumptions: what factors, for planning purposes, are you considering to be true?

34. When is a charter needed?

35. How do you manage integration?

36. Why do you need to manage scope?

37. How are Cloud Service Provider projects different from operations?

38. Success determination factors: how will the success of the Cloud Service Provider project be determined from the customers perspective?

39. Why Outsource?

40. Did your Cloud Service Provider project ask for this?

1.2 Stakeholder Register: Cloud Service Provider

41. What is the power of the stakeholder?

42. How will reports be created?

43. Who are the stakeholders?

44. What are the major Cloud Service Provider project milestones requiring communications or providing communications opportunities?

45. Is your organization ready for change?

46. What & Why?

47. Who is managing stakeholder engagement?

48. How should employers make voices heard?

49. What opportunities exist to provide communications?

50. Who wants to talk about Security?

51. How much influence do they have on the Cloud Service Provider project?

52. How big is the gap?

1.3 Stakeholder Analysis Matrix: Cloud Service Provider

53. Who has control over whom?

54. Gaps in capabilities?

55. Effects on core activities, distraction?

56. What are the key services, contractual arrangements, or other relationships between stakeholder groups?

57. Economy - home, abroad?

58. Why is it important to identify them?

59. Cashflow, start-up cash-drain?

60. Do recommendations include actions to address any differential distribution of impacts?

61. What can the Cloud Service Provider projects outcome be used for?

62. What actions can be taken to reduce or mitigate risk?

63. Who will be responsible for managing the outcome?

64. Who is most dependent on the resources at stake?

65. Who holds positions of responsibility in interested organizations?

66. Could any of your organizations weaknesses seriously threaten development?

67. If you can not fix it, how do you do it differently?

68. How can you counter negative efforts?

69. Marketing - reach, distribution, awareness?

70. How can you fill the need to show progress?

71. What is the stakeholders power and status in relation to the Cloud Service Provider project?

2.0 Planning Process Group: Cloud Service Provider

72. To what extent is the program helping to influence your organizations policy framework?

73. What makes your Cloud Service Provider project successful?

74. Are work methodologies, financial instruments, etc. shared among departments, organizations and Cloud Service Provider projects?

75. What is involved in Cloud Service Provider project scope management, and why is good Cloud Service Provider project scope management so important on information technology Cloud Service Provider projects?

76. How can you tell when you are done?

77. To what extent have public/private national resources and/or counterparts been mobilized to contribute to the programs objective and produce results and impacts?

78. Will the products created live up to the necessary quality?

79. Did the program design/ implementation strategy adequately address the planning stage necessary to set up structures, hire staff etc.?

80. In what way has the program contributed towards the issue culture and development included on the public agenda?

81. To what extent are the visions and actions of the partners consistent or divergent with regard to the program?

82. How will users learn how to use the deliverables?

83. Mitigate. what will you do to minimize the impact should a risk event occur?

84. How well will the chosen processes produce the expected results?

85. When will the Cloud Service Provider project be done?

86. Professionals want to know what is expected from them; what are the deliverables?

87. What is the difference between the early schedule and late schedule?

88. How are the principles of aid effectiveness (ownership, alignment, management for development results and mutual responsibility) being applied in the Cloud Service Provider project?

89. To what extent has a PMO contributed to raising the quality of the design of the Cloud Service Provider project?

90. How well do the team follow the chosen processes?

2.1 Project Management Plan: Cloud Service Provider

91. Is mitigation authorized or recommended?

92. Was the peer (technical) review of the cost estimates duly coordinated with the cost estimate center of expertise and addressed in the review documentation and certification?

93. Are alternatives safe, functional, constructible, economical, reasonable and sustainable?

94. Are cost risk analysis methods applied to develop contingencies for the estimated total Cloud Service Provider project costs?

95. How do you manage time?

96. Are comparable cost estimates used for comparing, screening and selecting alternative plans, and has a reasonable cost estimate been developed for the recommended plan?

97. What are the deliverables?

98. Where does all this information come from?

99. How do you organize the costs in the Cloud Service Provider project management plan?

100. What did not work so well?

101. Are there non-structural buyout or relocation recommendations?

102. Is there an incremental analysis/cost effectiveness analysis of proposed mitigation features based on an approved method and using an accepted model?

103. Is the budget realistic?

104. What went right?

105. Are the existing and future without-plan conditions reasonable and appropriate?

106. Are there any Client staffing expectations?

107. When is the Cloud Service Provider project management plan created?

108. What should you drop in order to add something new?

2.2 Scope Management Plan: Cloud Service Provider

109. Is the communication plan being followed?

110. Is pert / critical path or equivalent methodology being used?

111. Is there an approved case?

112. Are the quality tools and methods identified in the Quality Plan appropriate to the Cloud Service Provider project?

113. Are there procedures in place to effectively manage interdependencies with other Cloud Service Provider projects, systems, Vendors and your organizations work effort?

114. Are funding resource estimates sufficiently detailed and documented for use in planning and tracking the Cloud Service Provider project?

115. Are adequate resources provided for the quality assurance function?

116. Does a documented Cloud Service Provider project organizational policy & plan (i.e. governance model) exist?

117. Quality standards - are controls in place to ensure that the work was not only completed and also completed to meet specific standards?

118. Have key stakeholders been identified?

119. Are staffing resource estimates sufficiently detailed and documented for use in planning and tracking the Cloud Service Provider project?

120. What strengths do you have?

121. Pareto diagrams, statistical sampling, flow charting or trend analysis used quality monitoring?

122. Describe the manner in which Cloud Service Provider project deliverables will be formally presented and accepted. Will they be presented at the end of each phase?

123. To whom will the deliverables be first presented for inspection and verification?

124. Are software metrics formally captured, analyzed and used as a basis for other Cloud Service Provider project estimates?

125. How relevant is this attribute to this Cloud Service Provider project or audit?

126. Are the Cloud Service Provider project plans updated on a frequent basis?

127. Can each item be appropriately scheduled?

128. Are estimating assumptions and constraints captured?

2.3 Requirements Management Plan: Cloud Service Provider

129. What are you counting on?

130. What information regarding the Cloud Service Provider project requirements will be reported?

131. What performance metrics will be used?

132. Is there formal agreement on who has authority to request a change in requirements?

133. Business analysis scope?

134. Do you know which stakeholders will participate in the requirements effort?

135. Is stakeholder risk tolerance an important factor for the requirements process in this Cloud Service Provider project?

136. Who is responsible for monitoring and tracking the Cloud Service Provider project requirements?

137. Is requirements work dependent on any other specific Cloud Service Provider project or non-Cloud Service Provider project activities (e.g. funding, approvals, procurement)?

138. Has the requirements team been instructed in the Change Control process?

139. How will the information be distributed?

140. How will bidders price evaluations be done, by deliverables, phases, or in a big bang?

141. After the requirements are gathered and set forth on the requirements register, theyre little more than a laundry list of items. Some may be duplicates, some might conflict with others and some will be too broad or too vague to understand. Describe how the requirements will be analyzed. Who will perform the analysis?

142. Who will do the reporting and to whom will reports be delivered?

143. Which hardware or software, related to, or as outcome of the Cloud Service Provider project is new to your organization?

144. Did you use declarative statements?

145. Are all the stakeholders ready for the transition into the user community?

146. How will you develop the schedule of requirements activities?

147. Will you document changes to requirements?

148. Do you really need to write this document at all?

2.4 Requirements Documentation: Cloud Service Provider

149. How will the proposed Cloud Service Provider project help?

150. Is your business case still valid?

151. Is new technology needed?

152. How will requirements be documented and who signs off on them?

153. Do technical resources exist?

154. Does your organization restrict technical alternatives?

155. How does what is being described meet the business need?

156. What will be the integration problems?

157. What variations exist for a process?

158. Basic work/business process; high-level, what is being touched?

159. What if the system wasn t implemented?

160. How do you know when a Requirement is accurate enough?

161. The problem with gathering requirements is right there in the word gathering. What images does it conjure?

162. Who is interacting with the system?

163. What happens when requirements are wrong?

164. How much does requirements engineering cost?

165. Has requirements gathering uncovered information that would necessitate changes?

166. What kind of entity is a problem ?

167. What images does it conjure?

2.5 Requirements Traceability Matrix: Cloud Service Provider

168. How do you manage scope?

169. Why do you manage scope?

170. Will you use a Requirements Traceability Matrix?

171. What is the WBS?

172. How small is small enough?

173. What are the chronologies, contingencies, consequences, criteria?

174. Describe the process for approving requirements so they can be added to the traceability matrix and Cloud Service Provider project work can be performed. Will the Cloud Service Provider project requirements become approved in writing?

175. Do you have a clear understanding of all subcontracts in place?

176. How will it affect the stakeholders personally in career?

177. What percentage of Cloud Service Provider projects are producing traceability matrices between requirements and other work products?

178. Why use a WBS?

179. Is there a requirements traceability process in place?

2.6 Project Scope Statement: Cloud Service Provider

180. Is there an information system for the Cloud Service Provider project?

181. What are the defined meeting materials?

182. Are there completion/verification criteria defined for each task producing an output?

183. Is there a process (test plans, inspections, reviews) defined for verifying outputs for each task?

184. Identify how your team and you will create the Cloud Service Provider project scope statement and the work breakdown structure (WBS). Document how you will create the Cloud Service Provider project scope statement and WBS, and make sure you answer the following questions: In defining Cloud Service Provider project scope and the WBS, will you and your Cloud Service Provider project team be using methods defined by your organization, methods defined by the Cloud Service Provider project management office (PMO), or other methods?

185. How often do you estimate that the scope might change, and why?

186. Were key Cloud Service Provider project stakeholders brought into the Cloud Service Provider project Plan?

187. Is the plan for Cloud Service Provider project resources adequate?

188. Elements of scope management that deal with concept development ?

189. What is the most common tool for helping define the detail?

190. Does the scope statement still need some clarity?

191. Will you need a statement of work?

192. Is the quality function identified and assigned?

193. Is the Cloud Service Provider project sponsor function identified and defined?

194. Is there a Quality Assurance Plan documented and filed?

195. Elements that deal with providing the detail?

196. How will you verify the accuracy of the work of the Cloud Service Provider project, and what constitutes acceptance of the deliverables?

197. Have the reports to be produced, distributed, and filed been defined?

198. Where and how does the team fit within your organization structure?

2.7 Assumption and Constraint Log: Cloud Service Provider

199. Does the Cloud Service Provider project have a formal Cloud Service Provider project Plan?

200. Are there processes defining how software will be developed including development methods, overall timeline for development, software product standards, and traceability?

201. Has a Cloud Service Provider project Communications Plan been developed?

202. No superfluous information or marketing narrative?

203. Were the system requirements formally reviewed prior to initiating the design phase?

204. How many Cloud Service Provider project staff does this specific process affect?

205. Are there nonconformance issues?

206. Are funding and staffing resource estimates sufficiently detailed and documented for use in planning and tracking the Cloud Service Provider project?

207. Is there documentation of system capability requirements, data requirements, environment requirements, security requirements, and computer

and hardware requirements?

208. Have all stakeholders been identified?

209. Are there processes in place to ensure internal consistency between the source code components?

210. Have you eliminated all duplicative tasks or manual efforts, where appropriate?

211. Have all necessary approvals been obtained?

212. What do you audit?

213. How do you design an auditing system?

214. When can log be discarded?

215. Is there a Steering Committee in place?

216. Do the requirements meet the standards of correctness, completeness, consistency, accuracy, and readability?

217. Are requirements management tracking tools and procedures in place?

218. Contradictory information between different documents?

2.8 Work Breakdown Structure: Cloud Service Provider

219. How much detail?

220. Why would you develop a Work Breakdown Structure?

221. Is the work breakdown structure (wbs) defined and is the scope of the Cloud Service Provider project clear with assigned deliverable owners?

222. Do you need another level?

223. When does it have to be done?

224. What is the probability that the Cloud Service Provider project duration will exceed xx weeks?

225. Where does it take place?

226. How big is a work-package?

227. Is it a change in scope?

228. Why is it useful?

229. What is the probability of completing the Cloud Service Provider project in less that xx days?

230. When do you stop?

231. Who has to do it?

232. What has to be done?

233. How many levels?

234. When would you develop a Work Breakdown Structure?

235. Can you make it?

2.9 WBS Dictionary: Cloud Service Provider

236. Detailed schedules which support control account and work package start and completion dates/events?

237. The already stated responsible for overhead performance control of related costs?

238. Are overhead cost budgets (or Cloud Service Provider projections) established on a facility-wide basis at least annually for the life of the contract?

239. Intermediate schedules, as required, which provide a logical sequence from the master schedule to the control account level?

240. Is the anticipated (firm and potential) business base Cloud Service Provider projected in a rational, consistent manner?

241. Are procedures in existence that control replanning of unopened work packages, and are corresponding procedures adhered to?

242. Does the scheduling system provide for the identification of work progress against technical and other milestones, and also provide for forecasts of completion dates of scheduled work?

243. Are records maintained to show how undistributed budgets are controlled?

244. Are retroactive changes to direct costs and indirect costs prohibited except for the correction of errors and routine accounting adjustments?

245. The wbs is developed as part of a joint planning session. and how do you know that youhave done this right?

246. Are data elements (BCWS, BCWP, and ACWP) progressively summarized from the detail level to the contract level through the CWBS?

247. Are data being used by managers in an effective manner to ascertain Cloud Service Provider project or functional status, to identify reasons or significant variance, and to initiate appropriate corrective action?

248. Is all contract work included in the CWBS?

249. Are the responsibilities and authorities of each of the above organizational elements or managers clearly defined?

250. What is the end result of a work package?

251. Evaluate the performance of operating organizations?

252. Are the latest revised estimates of costs at completion compared with the established budgets at appropriate levels and causes of variances identified?

253. Where engineering standards or other internal work measurement systems are used, is there a formal

relationship between corresponding values and work package budgets?

254. Is cost and schedule performance measurement done in a consistent, systematic manner?

255. Are indirect costs accumulated for comparison with the corresponding budgets?

2.10 Schedule Management Plan: Cloud Service Provider

256. What happens if a warning is triggered?

257. Are written status reports provided on a designated frequent basis?

258. Does the business case include how the Cloud Service Provider project aligns with your organizations strategic goals & objectives?

259. Are Cloud Service Provider project team members committed fulltime?

260. Are changes in scope (deliverable commitments) agreed to by all affected groups & individuals?

261. Have the procedures for identifying budget variances been followed?

262. Is there anything planned that does not need to be here?

263. Are milestone deliverables effectively tracked and compared to Cloud Service Provider project plan?

264. Has the budget been baselined?

265. Has the Cloud Service Provider project scope been baselined?

266. Can additional resources be added to

subsequent tasks to reduce the durations of the already stated tasks?

267. Is a process for scheduling and reporting defined, including forms and formats?

268. Does the Cloud Service Provider project have a Quality Culture?

269. Does the detailed work plan match the complexity of tasks with the capabilities of personnel?

270. Are all resource assumptions documented?

271. Is the ims development and management approach described?

272. Is there any form of automated support for Issues Management?

273. Are action items captured and managed?

274. Has the scope management document been updated and distributed to help prevent scope creep?

2.11 Activity List: Cloud Service Provider

275. Is infrastructure setup part of your Cloud Service Provider project?

276. What will be performed?

277. Are the required resources available or need to be acquired?

278. How will it be performed?

279. How difficult will it be to do specific activities on this Cloud Service Provider project?

280. Should you include sub-activities?

281. How much slack is available in the Cloud Service Provider project?

282. Can you determine the activity that must finish, before this activity can start?

283. How can the Cloud Service Provider project be displayed graphically to better visualize the activities?

284. For other activities, how much delay can be tolerated?

285. What did not go as well?

286. When will the work be performed?

287. What are the critical bottleneck activities?

288. What is the probability the Cloud Service Provider project can be completed in xx weeks?

289. What is your organizations history in doing similar activities?

290. What went wrong?

291. What is the total time required to complete the Cloud Service Provider project if no delays occur?

2.12 Activity Attributes: Cloud Service Provider

292. Can you re-assign any activities to another resource to resolve an over-allocation?

293. How difficult will it be to do specific activities on this Cloud Service Provider project?

294. How many resources do you need to complete the work scope within a limit of X number of days?

295. Does your organization of the data change its meaning?

296. Time for overtime?

297. Activity: what is In the Bag?

298. What conclusions/generalizations can you draw from this?

299. What is the general pattern here?

300. Resource is assigned to?

301. Where else does it apply?

302. Were there other ways you could have organized the data to achieve similar results?

303. Are the required resources available?

304. Have constraints been applied to the start and finish milestones for the phases?

305. Is there a trend during the year?

306. Can more resources be added?

307. How else could the items be grouped?

308. Has management defined a definite timeframe for the turnaround or Cloud Service Provider project window?

2.13 Milestone List: Cloud Service Provider

309. Legislative effects?

310. Continuity, supply chain robustness?

311. Insurmountable weaknesses?

312. Milestone pages should display the UserID of the person who added the milestone. Does a report or query exist that provides this audit information?

313. It is to be a narrative text providing the crucial aspects of your Cloud Service Provider project proposal answering what, who, how, when and where?

314. How soon can the activity finish?

315. Identify critical paths (one or more) and which activities are on the critical path?

316. How late can the activity finish?

317. Environmental effects?

318. Loss of key staff?

319. Political effects?

320. Describe the industry you are in and the market growth opportunities. What is the market for your

technology, product or service?

321. When will the Cloud Service Provider project be complete?

322. Can you derive how soon can the whole Cloud Service Provider project finish?

323. Information and research?

324. How late can each activity be finished and started?

325. How will the milestone be verified?

2.14 Network Diagram: Cloud Service Provider

326. How difficult will it be to do specific activities on this Cloud Service Provider project?

327. Planning: who, how long, what to do?

328. What activities must follow this activity?

329. Are the gantt chart and/or network diagram updated periodically and used to assess the overall Cloud Service Provider project timetable?

330. What activities must occur simultaneously with this activity?

331. If a current contract exists, can you provide the vendor name, contract start, and contract expiration date?

332. Where do you schedule uncertainty time?

333. What job or jobs precede it?

334. What are the Key Success Factors?

335. Can you calculate the confidence level?

336. What controls the start and finish of a job?

337. Why must you schedule milestones, such as reviews, throughout the Cloud Service Provider

project?

338. If x is long, what would be the completion time if you break x into two parallel parts of y weeks and z weeks?

339. What to do and When?

340. Are you on time?

341. If the Cloud Service Provider project network diagram cannot change and you have extra personnel resources, what is the BEST thing to do?

342. Where do schedules come from?

343. What is the completion time?

344. What activity must be completed immediately before this activity can start?

2.15 Activity Resource Requirements: Cloud Service Provider

345. Are there unresolved issues that need to be addressed?

346. Which logical relationship does the PDM use most often?

347. When does monitoring begin?

348. What is the Work Plan Standard?

349. Do you use tools like decomposition and rolling-wave planning to produce the activity list and other outputs?

350. Anything else?

351. How do you handle petty cash?

352. Other support in specific areas?

353. Why do you do that?

354. Organizational Applicability?

355. What are constraints that you might find during the Human Resource Planning process?

356. How many signatures do you require on a check and does this match what is in your policy and procedures?

2.16 Resource Breakdown Structure: Cloud Service Provider

357. Who is allowed to perform which functions?

358. What is Cloud Service Provider project communication management?

359. What is the primary purpose of the human resource plan?

360. What are the requirements for resource data?

361. What is the purpose of assigning and documenting responsibility?

362. Who is allowed to see what data about which resources?

363. Which resources should be in the resource pool?

364. What defines a successful Cloud Service Provider project?

365. Why time management?

366. What is each stakeholders desired outcome for the Cloud Service Provider project?

367. Goals for the Cloud Service Provider project. What is each stakeholders desired outcome for the Cloud Service Provider project?

368. How should the information be delivered?

369. When do they need the information?

370. Any changes from stakeholders?

371. How difficult will it be to do specific activities on this Cloud Service Provider project?

372. Who needs what information?

373. Who delivers the information?

2.17 Activity Duration Estimates: Cloud Service Provider

374. Which is the BEST Cloud Service Provider project management tool to use to determine the longest time the Cloud Service Provider project will take?

375. Are contractor costs, schedule and technical performance monitored throughout the Cloud Service Provider project?

376. On which process should team members spend the most time?

377. Why is there a growing trend in outsourcing, especially in the government?

378. Does the software appear easy to learn?

379. Are reward and recognition systems defined to promote or reinforce desired behavior?

380. Which best describes how this affects the Cloud Service Provider project?

381. What is the difference between conceptual, application, and evaluative questions?

382. Are inspections completed to determine if the results comply with the requirements?

383. Is a Cloud Service Provider project charter created once a Cloud Service Provider project is

formally recognized?

384. What do you think the real problem was in this case?

385. Total slack can be calculated by which equations?

386. After changes are approved are Cloud Service Provider project documents updated and distributed?

387. Are adjustments implemented to correct or prevent defects?

388. When would a milestone chart be used instead of a bar char?

389. Consider the examples of poor quality in information technology Cloud Service Provider projects presented in the What Went Wrong?

390. What is pmp certification, and why do you think the number of people earning it has grown so much in the past ten years?

391. How does Cloud Service Provider project management relate to other disciplines?

392. Consider the changes in the job market for information technology workers. How does the job market and current state of the economy affect human resource management?

393. What are key inputs and outputs of the software?

2.18 Duration Estimating Worksheet: Cloud Service Provider

394. What utility impacts are there?

395. When do the individual activities need to start and finish?

396. When, then?

397. Does the Cloud Service Provider project provide innovative ways for stakeholders to overcome obstacles or deliver better outcomes?

398. Small or large Cloud Service Provider project?

399. What is the total time required to complete the Cloud Service Provider project if no delays occur?

400. How can the Cloud Service Provider project be displayed graphically to better visualize the activities?

401. Is the Cloud Service Provider project responsive to community need?

402. What is next?

403. What questions do you have?

404. How should ongoing costs be monitored to try to keep the Cloud Service Provider project within budget?

405. Will the Cloud Service Provider project collaborate with the local community and leverage resources?

406. Done before proceeding with this activity or what can be done concurrently?

407. Is this operation cost effective?

408. Value pocket identification & quantification what are value pockets?

409. Science = process: remember the scientific method?

410. Why estimate time and cost?

2.19 Project Schedule: Cloud Service Provider

411. Why is this particularly bad?

412. Does the condition or event threaten the Cloud Service Provider projects objectives in any ways?

413. How do you know that youhave done this right?

414. Meet requirements?

415. Are there activities that came from a template or previous Cloud Service Provider project that are not applicable on this phase of this Cloud Service Provider project?

416. How do you use schedules?

417. How effectively were issues able to be resolved without impacting the Cloud Service Provider project Schedule or Budget?

418. Are procedures defined by which the Cloud Service Provider project schedule may be changed?

419. Did the Cloud Service Provider project come in under budget?

420. Schedule/cost recovery?

421. Have all Cloud Service Provider project delays been adequately accounted for, communicated to all

stakeholders and adjustments made in overall Cloud Service Provider project schedule?

422. Are the original Cloud Service Provider project schedule and budget realistic?

423. Your Cloud Service Provider project management plan results in a Cloud Service Provider project schedule that is too long. If the Cloud Service Provider project network diagram cannot change and you have extra personnel resources, what is the BEST thing to do?

424. Why is software Cloud Service Provider project disaster so common?

425. What is Cloud Service Provider project management?

426. Did the Cloud Service Provider project come in on schedule?

427. Understand the constraints used in preparing the schedule. Are activities connected because logic dictates the order in which others occur?

428. How does a Cloud Service Provider project get to be a year late ?

2.20 Cost Management Plan: Cloud Service Provider

429. Have Cloud Service Provider project team accountabilities & responsibilities been clearly defined?

430. Is it standard practice to formally commit stakeholders to the Cloud Service Provider project via agreements?

431. Are any non-compliance issues that exist due to State practices communicated to your organization?

432. Has Cloud Service Provider project success criteria been defined?

433. What is Cloud Service Provider project cost management?

434. Are decisions captured in a decisions log?

435. Timeline and milestones?

436. Were stakeholders aware and supportive of the principles and practices of modern software estimation?

437. Forecasts – how will the time and resources needed to complete the Cloud Service Provider project be forecast?

438. What weaknesses do you have?

439. Exclusions – is there scope to be performed or provided by others?

440. What is cost and Cloud Service Provider project cost management?

441. Is there an onboarding process in place?

442. The definition of the Cloud Service Provider project scope what needs to be accomplished?

443. Is Cloud Service Provider project work proceeding in accordance with the original Cloud Service Provider project schedule?

444. Is it a Cloud Service Provider project?

445. Are Cloud Service Provider project leaders committed to this Cloud Service Provider project full time?

446. Is there an on-going process in place to monitor Cloud Service Provider project risks?

447. Is there anything unique in this Cloud Service Provider projects scope statement that will affect resources?

448. Have adequate resources been provided by management to ensure Cloud Service Provider project success?

2.21 Activity Cost Estimates: Cloud Service Provider

449. Does the activity rely on a common set of tools to carry it out?

450. What cost data should be used to estimate costs during the 2-year follow-up period?

451. What procedures are put in place regarding bidding and cost comparisons, if any?

452. How do you change activities?

453. Are cost subtotals needed?

454. What is the Cloud Service Provider projects sustainability strategy that will ensure Cloud Service Provider project results will endure or be sustained?

455. Will you need to provide essential services information about activities?

456. How do you fund change orders?

457. What were things that you did well, and could improve, and how?

458. How many activities should you have?

459. What communication items need improvement?

460. Were the tasks or work products prepared by the

consultant useful?

461. Padding is bad and contingencies are good. what is the difference?

462. Did the Cloud Service Provider project team have the right skills?

463. What is the activity recast of the budget?

464. What makes a good expected result statement?

465. One way to define activities is to consider how organization employees describe jobs to families and friends. You basically want to know, What do you do?

466. What is a Cloud Service Provider project Management Plan?

2.22 Cost Estimating Worksheet: Cloud Service Provider

467. Does the Cloud Service Provider project provide innovative ways for stakeholders to overcome obstacles or deliver better outcomes?

468. What info is needed?

469. Can a trend be established from historical performance data on the selected measure and are the criteria for using trend analysis or forecasting methods met?

470. Identify the timeframe necessary to monitor progress and collect data to determine how the selected measure has changed?

471. What is the estimated labor cost today based upon this information?

472. Who is best positioned to know and assist in identifying corresponding factors?

473. What is the purpose of estimating?

474. What additional Cloud Service Provider project(s) could be initiated as a result of this Cloud Service Provider project?

475. Is the Cloud Service Provider project responsive to community need?

476. Will the Cloud Service Provider project collaborate with the local community and leverage resources?

477. Is it feasible to establish a control group arrangement?

478. What will others want?

479. How will the results be shared and to whom?

480. What costs are to be estimated?

481. Ask: are others positioned to know, are others credible, and will others cooperate?

482. What can be included?

483. What happens to any remaining funds not used?

2.23 Cost Baseline: Cloud Service Provider

484. On budget?

485. At which frequency ?

486. Have the lessons learned been filed with the Cloud Service Provider project Management Office?

487. Has training and knowledge transfer of the operations organization been completed?

488. How fast?

489. Who will use corresponding metrics ?

490. What is the consequence?

491. Are you asking management for something as a result of this update?

492. If you sold 10x widgets on a day, what would the affect on profits be?

493. Does a process exist for establishing a cost baseline to measure Cloud Service Provider project performance?

494. What does a good WBS NOT look like?

495. How will cost estimates be used?

496. Cloud Service Provider project goals -should others be reconsidered?

497. What would the life cycle costs be?

498. Have you identified skills that are missing from your team?

499. Has operations management formally accepted responsibility for operating and maintaining the product(s) or service(s) delivered by the Cloud Service Provider project?

500. Are you meeting with your team regularly?

501. Are there contingencies or conditions related to the acceptance?

2.24 Quality Management Plan: Cloud Service Provider

502. You know what your customers expectations are regarding this process?

503. What are your organizations current levels and trends for the already stated measures related to employee wellbeing, satisfaction, and development?

504. Sampling part of task?

505. Does the Cloud Service Provider project have a formal Cloud Service Provider project Plan?

506. How are people conducting sampling trained?

507. Are best practices and metrics employed to identify issues, progress, performance, etc.?

508. How are corresponding standards measured?

509. What are your organizations current levels and trends for the already stated measures related to customer satisfaction/ dissatisfaction and product/ service performance?

510. What procedures are used to determine if you use, and the number of split, replicate or duplicate samples taken at a site?

511. How do you ensure that your sampling methods and procedures meet your data quality objectives?

512. How are your organizations compensation and recognition approaches and the performance management system used to reinforce high performance?

513. How does your organization recruit, hire, and retain new employees?

514. What else should you do now?

515. How do senior leaders review organizational performance?

516. How does your organization decide what to measure?

517. Methodology followed?

518. How are calibration records kept?

519. How do you field-modify testing procedures?

520. How does training support what is important to your organization and the individual?

2.25 Quality Metrics: Cloud Service Provider

521. How does one achieve stability?

522. How do you calculate corresponding metrics?

523. Is there a set of procedures to capture, analyze and act on quality metrics?

524. Are there already quality metrics available that detect nonlinear embeddings and trends similar to the users perception?

525. Have risk areas been identified?

526. How do you know if everyone is trying to improve the right things?

527. What are you trying to accomplish?

528. Who notifies stakeholders of normal and abnormal results?

529. How should customers provide input?

530. What documentation is required?

531. What is the benchmark?

532. Why is now the time for quality metrics?

533. Subjective quality component: customer

satisfaction, how do you measure it?

534. What forces exist that would cause them to change?

535. Product Availability ?

536. What approved evidence based screening tools can be used?

537. How effective are your security tests?

538. Should a modifier be included?

539. What happens if you get an abnormal result?

2.26 Process Improvement Plan: Cloud Service Provider

540. Modeling current processes is great, and will you ever see a return on that investment?

541. Why quality management?

542. Why do you want to achieve the goal?

543. Where are you now?

544. Where do you want to be?

545. Does your process ensure quality?

546. What is the return on investment?

547. What personnel are the sponsors for that initiative?

548. Are you making progress on the improvement framework?

549. Have storage and access mechanisms and procedures been determined?

550. Everyone agrees on what process improvement is, right?

551. Does explicit definition of the measures exist?

552. How do you manage quality?

553. Have the supporting tools been developed or acquired?

554. Are you following the quality standards?

555. What personnel are the change agents for your initiative?

556. Are you meeting the quality standards?

557. Are you making progress on the goals?

558. Has the time line required to move measurement results from the points of collection to databases or users been established?

559. What is quality and how will you ensure it?

2.27 Responsibility Assignment Matrix: Cloud Service Provider

560. Do you need to convince people that its well worth the time and effort?

561. What are the assumptions?

562. Performance to date and material commitment?

563. Who is the sponsor?

564. Contemplated overhead expenditure for each period based on the best information currently available?

565. Contract line items and end items?

566. How can this help you with team building?

567. How do you manage remotely to staff in other Divisions?

568. Are your organizations and items of cost assigned to each pool identified?

569. What do you do when people do not respond?

570. Identify potential or actual overruns and underruns?

571. Which resource planning tool provides information on resource responsibility and

accountability?

572. Are the requirements for all items of overhead established by rational, traceable processes?

573. Too many as: does a proper segregation of duties exist?

574. Who is going to do that work?

575. Do all the identified groups or people really need to be consulted?

2.28 Roles and Responsibilities: Cloud Service Provider

576. What should you do now to ensure that you are exceeding expectations and excelling in your current position?

577. Attainable / achievable: the goal is attainable; can you actually accomplish the goal?

578. What is working well?

579. Are your budgets supportive of a culture of quality data?

580. Is there a training program in place for stakeholders covering expectations, roles and responsibilities and any addition knowledge others need to be good stakeholders?

581. To decide whether to use a quality measurement, ask how will you know when it is achieved?

582. What should you highlight for improvement?

583. Be specific; avoid generalities. Thank you and great work alone are insufficient. What exactly do you appreciate and why?

584. Is the data complete?

585. Once the responsibilities are defined for the Cloud Service Provider project, have the deliverables,

roles and responsibilities been clearly communicated to every participant?

586. Are governance roles and responsibilities documented?

587. Required skills, knowledge, experience?

588. Are Cloud Service Provider project team roles and responsibilities identified and documented?

589. What expectations were NOT met?

590. Was the expectation clearly communicated?

591. What expectations were met?

592. What specific behaviors did you observe?

2.29 Human Resource Management Plan: Cloud Service Provider

593. Is it standard practice to formally commit stakeholders to the Cloud Service Provider project via agreements?

594. What were things that you did very well and want to do the same again on the next Cloud Service Provider project?

595. Account for the purpose of this Cloud Service Provider project by describing, at a high-level, what will be done. What is this Cloud Service Provider project aiming to achieve?

596. How to convince employees that this is a necessary process?

597. Is your organization certified as a supplier, wholesaler, regular dealer, or manufacturer of corresponding products/supplies?

598. Are vendor contract reports, reviews and visits conducted periodically?

599. What commitments have been made?

600. Were escalated issues resolved promptly?

601. Does the resource management plan include a personnel development plan?

602. Are the schedule estimates reasonable given the Cloud Service Provider project?

603. Who needs training?

604. Are meeting minutes captured and sent out after the meeting?

605. Is it possible to track all classes of Cloud Service Provider project work (e.g. scheduled, un-scheduled, defect repair, etc.)?

606. Are the payment terms being followed?

607. How relevant is this attribute to this Cloud Service Provider project or audit?

608. Is documentation created for communication with the suppliers and Vendors?

609. What were things that you need to improve?

610. Are the Cloud Service Provider project plans updated on a frequent basis?

611. Are updated Cloud Service Provider project time & resource estimates reasonable based on the current Cloud Service Provider project stage?

2.30 Communications Management Plan: Cloud Service Provider

612. Who are the members of the governing body?

613. What to know?

614. Who is the stakeholder?

615. Are stakeholders internal or external?

616. What help do you and your team need from the stakeholder?

617. Which stakeholders are thought leaders, influences, or early adopters?

618. Conflict resolution -which method when?

619. How much time does it take to do it?

620. What is the stakeholders level of authority?

621. What is the political influence?

622. How is this initiative related to other portfolios, programs, or Cloud Service Provider projects?

623. Do you prepare stakeholder engagement plans?

624. What is Cloud Service Provider project communications management?

625. Which stakeholders can influence others?

626. How do you manage communications?

627. Is there an important stakeholder who is actively opposed and will not receive messages?

628. Who needs to know and how much?

629. Which team member will work with each stakeholder?

630. In your work, how much time is spent on stakeholder identification?

631. How did the term stakeholder originate?

2.31 Risk Management Plan: Cloud Service Provider

632. Are certain activities taking a long time to complete?

633. What is the cost to the Cloud Service Provider project if it does occur?

634. Do requirements demand the use of new analysis, design, or testing methods?

635. Are the reports useful and easy to read?

636. How is risk response planning performed?

637. Where do risks appear in the business phases?

638. How is risk monitoring performed?

639. Methodology: how will risk management be performed on this Cloud Service Provider project?

640. What things are likely to change?

641. Do requirements put excessive performance constraints on the product?

642. Anticipated volatility of the requirements?

643. Are requirements fully understood by the software engineering team and customers?

644. Litigation – what is the probability that lawsuits will cause problems or delays in the Cloud Service Provider project?

645. Is this an issue, action item, question or a risk?

646. Are Cloud Service Provider project requirements stable?

647. Have top software and customer managers formally committed to support the Cloud Service Provider project?

648. Costs associated with late delivery or a defective product?

649. Is the customer willing to participate in reviews?

650. Why do you want risk management?

2.32 Risk Register: Cloud Service Provider

651. What may happen or not go according to plan?

652. Is further information required before making a decision?

653. What is a Risk?

654. Budget and schedule: what are the estimated costs and schedules for performing risk-related activities?

655. Having taken action, how did the responses effect change, and where is the Cloud Service Provider project now?

656. What can be done about it?

657. What is the appropriate level of risk management for this Cloud Service Provider project?

658. How are risks identified?

659. Methodology: how will risk management be performed on this Cloud Service Provider project?

660. What risks might negatively or positively affect achieving the Cloud Service Provider project objectives?

661. What is the reason for current performance

gaps and do the risks and opportunities identified previously account for this?

662. When is it going to be done?

663. Technology risk -is the Cloud Service Provider project technically feasible?

664. Can the likelihood and impact of failing to achieve corresponding recommendations and action plans be assessed?

665. What is your current and future risk profile?

666. User involvement: do you have the right users?

667. Schedule impact/severity estimated range (workdays) assume the event happens, what is the potential impact?

668. When will it happen?

669. Recovery actions - planned actions taken once a risk has occurred to allow you to move on. What should you do after?

670. What are the assumptions and current status that support the assessment of the risk?

2.33 Probability and Impact Assessment: Cloud Service Provider

671. What should be the level of coordination?

672. What will be the likely political situation during the life of the Cloud Service Provider project?

673. What should be done with non-critical risks?

674. Is the customer willing to commit significant time to the requirements gathering process?

675. Prioritized components/features?

676. What are the current or emerging trends of culture?

677. What can you do to minimize the impact if it does?

678. Are staff committed for the duration of the Cloud Service Provider project?

679. Are the risk data complete?

680. Who are the international/overseas Cloud Service Provider project partners (equipment supplier/supplier/consultant/contractor) for this Cloud Service Provider project?

681. Can you stabilize dynamic risk factors?

682. Has something like this been done before?

683. What action do you usually take against risks?

684. Is security a central objective?

685. What are the likely future requirements?

686. What will be the likely political environment during the life of the Cloud Service Provider project?

687. What would be the effect of slippage?

688. Do you have a consistent repeatable process that is actually used?

689. Have you ascribed a level of confidence to every critical technical objective?

690. Is there additional information that would make you more confident about your analysis?

2.34 Probability and Impact Matrix: Cloud Service Provider

691. How realistic is the timing of introduction?

692. Have you worked with the customer in the past?

693. Who should be notified of the occurrence of each of the risk indicators?

694. What changes in the regulation are forthcoming?

695. During Cloud Service Provider project executing, a team member identifies a risk that is not in the risk register. What should you do?

696. What are the methods to deal with risks?

697. What can go wrong?

698. To what extent is the chosen technology maturing?

699. Have customers been involved fully in the definition of requirements?

700. Which role do you have in the Cloud Service Provider project?

701. Are testing tools available and suitable?

702. Pay attention to the quality of the plans: is the content complete, or does it seem to be lacking

detail?

703. Do the requirements require the creation of new algorithms?

704. Workarounds are determined during which risk management process?

705. Do you need a risk management plan?

706. How well is the risk understood?

707. How much is the probability of the risk occurring?

2.35 Risk Data Sheet: Cloud Service Provider

708. How can hazards be reduced?

709. What can you do?

710. Has the most cost-effective solution been chosen?

711. Whom do you serve (customers)?

712. What are the main threats to your existence?

713. What is the chance that it will happen?

714. What can happen?

715. Who has a vested interest in how you perform as your organization (our stakeholders)?

716. What if client refuses?

717. Risk of what?

718. What was measured?

719. Has a sensitivity analysis been carried out?

720. What actions can be taken to eliminate or remove risk?

721. What are you trying to achieve (Objectives)?

722. Are new hazards created?

723. How do you handle product safely?

724. What do you know?

725. What are you here for (Mission)?

726. What will be the consequences if the risk happens?

2.36 Procurement Management Plan: Cloud Service Provider

727. Is Cloud Service Provider project status reviewed with the steering and executive teams at appropriate intervals?

728. Are Cloud Service Provider project contact logs kept up to date?

729. Does the Cloud Service Provider project have a Statement of Work?

730. Have lessons learned been conducted after each Cloud Service Provider project release?

731. What is the last item a Cloud Service Provider project manager must do to finalize Cloud Service Provider project close-out?

732. Has the business need been clearly defined?

733. Is there an issues management plan in place?

734. Does a documented Cloud Service Provider project organizational policy & plan (i.e. governance model) exist?

735. Why is procurement planning important?

736. Is the Cloud Service Provider project schedule available for all Cloud Service Provider project team members to review?

737. Are multiple estimation methods being employed?

738. Do Cloud Service Provider project managers participating in the Cloud Service Provider project know the Cloud Service Provider projects true status first hand?

739. Is the steering committee active in Cloud Service Provider project oversight?

740. Have all unresolved risks been documented?

741. Is Cloud Service Provider project work proceeding in accordance with the original Cloud Service Provider project schedule?

742. Is quality monitored from the perspective of the customers needs and expectations?

2.37 Source Selection Criteria: Cloud Service Provider

743. What are the special considerations for preaward debriefings?

744. What can not be disclosed?

745. Are types/quantities of material, facilities appropriate?

746. What should a DRFP include?

747. Do you consider all weaknesses, significant weaknesses, and deficiencies?

748. Do proposed hours support content and schedule?

749. Which contract type places the most risk on the seller?

750. Do you prepare an independent cost estimate?

751. In order of importance, which evaluation criteria are the most critical to the determination of your overall rating?

752. How should the oral presentations be handled?

753. Is a cost realism analysis used?

754. What should communications be used to

accomplish?

755. What information may not be provided?

756. What documentation is needed for a tradeoff decision?

757. How is past performance evaluated?

758. Is a letter of commitment from each proposed team member and key subcontractor included?

759. Are there any specific considerations that precludes offers from being selected as the awardee?

760. What risks were identified in the proposals?

761. Do you want to wait until all offerors have been evaluated?

762. What is cost analysis and when should it be performed?

2.38 Stakeholder Management Plan: Cloud Service Provider

763. Who might be involved in developing a charter?

764. Have Cloud Service Provider project management standards and procedures been established and documented?

765. Are there standards for code development?

766. Are updated Cloud Service Provider project time & resource estimates reasonable based on the current Cloud Service Provider project stage?

767. Are parking lot items captured?

768. What is to be the method of release?

769. Are all payments made according to the contract(s)?

770. What is the primary function of the Activity Decomposition Decision Tree?

771. Are Cloud Service Provider project leaders committed to this Cloud Service Provider project full time?

772. Is the amount of effort justified by the anticipated value of forming a new process?

773. Are formal code reviews conducted?

774. Does the Cloud Service Provider project have a formal Cloud Service Provider project Plan?

775. Is the performance of the supplier to be rated and documented?

776. Are cause and effect determined for risks when they occur?

777. Are meeting objectives identified for each meeting?

778. What is positive about the current process?

779. Has a resource management plan been created?

780. Are all key components of a Quality Assurance Plan present?

2.39 Change Management Plan: Cloud Service Provider

781. What are you trying to achieve as a result of communication?

782. What are the dependencies?

783. What processes are in place to manage knowledge about the Cloud Service Provider project?

784. Do there need to be new channels developed?

785. Have the business unit contacts been briefed by the Cloud Service Provider project team?

786. How do you gain sponsors buy-in to the communication plan?

787. Are there resource implications for your communications strategy?

788. Have the business unit contacts been selected and notified?

789. When should a given message be communicated?

790. What new roles are needed?

791. Why would a Cloud Service Provider project run more smoothly when change management is emphasized from the beginning?

792. Do you need new systems?

793. Does this change represent a completely new process for your organization, or a different application of an existing process?

794. Who will do the training?

795. How can you best frame the message so that it addresses the audiences interests?

796. What are the training strategies?

797. What risks may occur upfront?

798. What relationships will change?

799. Has this been negotiated with the customer and sponsor?

3.0 Executing Process Group: Cloud Service Provider

800. Who will provide training?

801. When is the appropriate time to bring the scorecard to Board meetings?

802. After how many days will the lease cost be the same as the purchase cost for the equipment?

803. Is the Cloud Service Provider project performing better or worse than planned?

804. Do schedule issues conflicts?

805. Who will be the main sponsor?

806. What areas does the group agree are the biggest success on the Cloud Service Provider project?

807. Will outside resources be needed to help?

808. Are escalated issues resolved promptly?

809. What good practices or successful experiences or transferable examples have been identified?

810. How many different communication channels does the Cloud Service Provider project team have?

811. Is the Cloud Service Provider project making progress in helping to achieve the set results?

812. Is the schedule for the set products being met?

813. Do the partners have sufficient financial capacity to keep up the benefits produced by the programme?

814. What areas were overlooked on this Cloud Service Provider project?

815. What is the product of your Cloud Service Provider project?

816. How do you enter durations, link tasks, and view critical path information?

817. How does Cloud Service Provider project management relate to other disciplines?

818. Do your results resemble a normal distribution?

3.1 Team Member Status Report: Cloud Service Provider

819. How will resource planning be done?

820. How it is to be done?

821. Why is it to be done?

822. How does this product, good, or service meet the needs of the Cloud Service Provider project and your organization as a whole?

823. Do you have an Enterprise Cloud Service Provider project Management Office (EPMO)?

824. What is to be done?

825. Are your organizations Cloud Service Provider projects more successful over time?

826. When a teams productivity and success depend on collaboration and the efficient flow of information, what generally fails them?

827. What specific interest groups do you have in place?

828. Does your organization have the means (staff, money, contract, etc.) to produce or to acquire the product, good, or service?

829. Are the attitudes of staff regarding Cloud Service

Provider project work improving?

830. The problem with Reward & Recognition Programs is that the truly deserving people all too often get left out. How can you make it practical?

831. How can you make it practical?

832. Will the staff do training or is that done by a third party?

833. How much risk is involved?

834. Does every department have to have a Cloud Service Provider project Manager on staff?

835. Does the product, good, or service already exist within your organization?

836. Are the products of your organizations Cloud Service Provider projects meeting customers objectives?

837. Is there evidence that staff is taking a more professional approach toward management of your organizations Cloud Service Provider projects?

3.2 Change Request: Cloud Service Provider

838. Are there requirements attributes that are strongly related to the occurrence of defects and failures?

839. Should a more thorough impact analysis be conducted?

840. What is the relationship between requirements attributes and reliability?

841. Will there be a change request form in use?

842. How are changes requested (forms, method of communication)?

843. How does your organization control changes before and after software is released to a customer?

844. What are the duties of the change control team?

845. What needs to be communicated?

846. Can static requirements change attributes like the size of the change be used to predict reliability in execution?

847. What is a Change Request Form?

848. Can you answer what happened, who did it, when did it happen, and what else will be affected?

849. Will all change requests be unconditionally tracked through this process?

850. Who can suggest changes?

851. What has an inspector to inspect and to check?

852. Which requirements attributes affect the risk to reliability the most?

853. Will new change requests be acknowledged in a timely manner?

854. Are there requirements attributes that can discriminate between high and low reliability?

855. Who has responsibility for approving and ranking changes?

856. For which areas does this operating procedure apply?

3.3 Change Log: Cloud Service Provider

857. Does the suggested change request represent a desired enhancement to the products functionality?

858. Is this a mandatory replacement?

859. When was the request approved?

860. Is the requested change request a result of changes in other Cloud Service Provider project(s)?

861. Is the change request open, closed or pending?

862. How does this change affect the timeline of the schedule?

863. Where do changes come from?

864. Does the suggested change request seem to represent a necessary enhancement to the product?

865. How does this relate to the standards developed for specific business processes?

866. How does this change affect scope?

867. When was the request submitted?

868. Who initiated the change request?

869. Will the Cloud Service Provider project fail if the

change request is not executed?

870. Is the submitted change a new change or a modification of a previously approved change?

871. Do the described changes impact on the integrity or security of the system?

872. Is the change backward compatible without limitations?

873. Is the change request within Cloud Service Provider project scope?

3.4 Decision Log: Cloud Service Provider

874. Is everything working as expected?

875. Behaviors; what are guidelines that the team has identified that will assist them with getting the most out of team meetings?

876. How do you define success?

877. How consolidated and comprehensive a story can you tell by capturing currently available incident data in a central location and through a log of key decisions during an incident?

878. What makes you different or better than others companies selling the same thing?

879. Adversarial environment. is your opponent open to a non-traditional workflow, or will it likely challenge anything you do?

880. It becomes critical to track and periodically revisit both operational effectiveness; Are you noticing all that you need to, and are you interpreting what you see effectively?

881. Decision-making process; how will the team make decisions?

882. What eDiscovery problem or issue did your organization set out to fix or make better?

883. How does provision of information, both in terms of content and presentation, influence acceptance of alternative strategies?

884. Who is the decisionmaker?

885. What is the average size of your matters in an applicable measurement?

886. What are the cost implications?

887. With whom was the decision shared or considered?

888. How do you know when you are achieving it?

889. Do strategies and tactics aimed at less than full control reduce the costs of management or simply shift the cost burden?

890. Which variables make a critical difference?

891. What was the rationale for the decision?

892. What is your overall strategy for quality control / quality assurance procedures?

893. How does an increasing emphasis on cost containment influence the strategies and tactics used?

3.5 Quality Audit: Cloud Service Provider

894. How does your organization know that its Mission, Vision and Values Statements are appropriate and effectively guiding your organization?

895. How does your organization know that its public relations and marketing systems are appropriately effective and constructive?

896. Are all employees including salespersons made aware that they must report all complaints received from any source for inclusion in the complaint handling system?

897. What is the collective experience of the team to be assigned to an audit?

898. How does your organization know that its staff have appropriate access to a fair and effective grievance process?

899. Are complaint files maintained?

900. Are measuring and test equipment that have been placed out of service suitably identified and excluded from use in any device reconditioning operation?

901. Is there a written corporate quality policy?

902. Are all employees made aware of device defects

which may occur from the improper performance of specific jobs?

903. How are you auditing your organizations compliance with regulations?

904. How does your organization know that its staff embody the core knowledge, skills and characteristics for which it wishes to be recognized?

905. How does your organization know that the system for managing its facilities is appropriately effective and constructive?

906. How does your organization know that its policy management system is appropriately effective and constructive?

907. How does your organization know that its system for examining work done is appropriately effective and constructive?

908. How does your organization know that its system for governing staff behaviour is appropriately effective and constructive?

909. Is refuse and garbage adequately stored and disposed of with sufficient frequency to prevent contamination?

910. Do prior clients have a positive opinion of your organization?

911. How does your organization know that the review processes are effective?

912. How does your organization know that its staff placements are appropriately effective and constructive in relation to program-related learning outcomes?

913. How does your organization know that the support for its staff is appropriately effective and constructive?

3.6 Team Directory: Cloud Service Provider

914. Who are your stakeholders (customers, sponsors, end users, team members)?

915. Contract requirements complied with?

916. Who will talk to the customer?

917. Who will write the meeting minutes and distribute?

918. Who will be the stakeholders on your next Cloud Service Provider project?

919. Process decisions: are all start-up, turn over and close out requirements of the contract satisfied?

920. Where should the information be distributed?

921. Why is the work necessary?

922. Have you decided when to celebrate the Cloud Service Provider projects completion date?

923. Timing: when do the effects of communication take place?

924. When will you produce deliverables?

925. How do unidentified risks impact the outcome of the Cloud Service Provider project?

926. Where will the product be used and/or delivered or built when appropriate?

927. Who should receive information (all stakeholders)?

928. Decisions: is the most suitable form of contract being used?

929. When does information need to be distributed?

930. How will you accomplish and manage the objectives?

931. Does a Cloud Service Provider project team directory list all resources assigned to the Cloud Service Provider project?

932. Decisions: what could be done better to improve the quality of the constructed product?

3.7 Team Operating Agreement: Cloud Service Provider

933. How will your group handle planned absences?

934. Are there more than two national cultures represented by your team?

935. Do you ensure that all participants know how to use the required technology?

936. How will you resolve conflict efficiently and respectfully?

937. To whom do you deliver your services?

938. What is the anticipated procedure (recruitment, solicitation of volunteers, or assignment) for selecting team members?

939. What is teaming?

940. Is compensation based on team and individual performance?

941. Do you brief absent members after they view meeting notes or listen to a recording?

942. Are there influences outside the team that may affect performance, and if so, have you identified and addressed them?

943. What are some potential sources of conflict

among team members?

944. How do you want to be thought of and known within your organization?

945. Do you solicit member feedback about meetings and what would make them better?

946. What individual strengths does each team member bring to the group?

947. What are the boundaries (organizational or geographic) within which you operate?

948. What are the safety issues/risks that need to be addressed and/or that the team needs to consider?

949. Must your team members rely on the expertise of other members to complete tasks?

950. Are there the right people on your team?

951. How will you divide work equitably?

952. Are there more than two functional areas represented by your team?

3.8 Team Performance Assessment: Cloud Service Provider

953. If you have criticized someones work for method variance in your role as reviewer, what was the circumstance?

954. How hard do you try to make a good selection?

955. To what degree are the skill areas critical to team performance present?

956. How do you keep key people outside the group informed about its accomplishments?

957. How hard did you try to make a good selection?

958. To what degree do members understand and articulate the same purpose without relying on ambiguous abstractions?

959. What are you doing specifically to develop the leaders around you?

960. To what degree are the goals realistic?

961. To what degree do members articulate the goals beyond the team membership?

962. Lack of method variance in self-reported affect and perceptions at work: Reality or artifact?

963. How much interpersonal friction is there in your

team?

964. To what degree will the team ensure that all members equitably share the work essential to the success of the team?

965. To what degree does the teams work approach provide opportunity for members to engage in results-based evaluation?

966. What are teams?

967. To what degree does the teams work approach provide opportunity for members to engage in fact-based problem solving?

968. To what degree can the team ensure that all members are individually and jointly accountable for the teams purpose, goals, approach, and work-products?

969. To what degree are the goals ambitious?

970. To what degree do all members feel responsible for all agreed-upon measures?

971. To what degree does the teams approach to its work allow for modification and improvement over time?

972. What makes opportunities more or less obvious?

3.9 Team Member Performance Assessment: Cloud Service Provider

973. For what period of time is a member rated?

974. What are best practices for delivering and developing training evaluations to maximize the benefits of leveraging emerging technologies?

975. What are top priorities?

976. Are the draft goals SMART ?

977. How are training activities developed from a technical perspective?

978. What is used as a basis for instructional decisions?

979. What evaluation results did you have?

980. To what degree do team members frequently explore the teams purpose and its implications?

981. What is needed for effective data teams?

982. How do you start collaborating?

983. To what degree does the team possess adequate membership to achieve its ends?

984. What, if any, steps are available for employees who feel they have been unfairly or inaccurately

rated?

985. What resources do you need?

986. How are performance measures and associated incentives developed?

987. To what degree can team members frequently and easily communicate with one another?

988. Who is responsible?

989. What happens if a team member receives a Rating of Unsatisfactory?

990. What is a general description of the processes under performance measurement and assessment?

991. How do you use data to inform instruction and improve staff achievement?

3.10 Issue Log: Cloud Service Provider

992. What are the typical contents?

993. What is the impact on the Business Case?

994. Who reported the issue?

995. Are there potential barriers between the team and the stakeholder?

996. Where do team members get information?

997. Who is involved as you identify stakeholders?

998. Are there too many who have an interest in some aspect of your work?

999. Who do you turn to if you have questions?

1000. What approaches do you use?

1001. How were past initiatives successful?

1002. Can an impact cause deviation beyond team, stage or Cloud Service Provider project tolerances?

1003. Are the Cloud Service Provider project issues uniquely identified, including to which product they refer?

1004. How is this initiative related to other portfolios, programs, or Cloud Service Provider projects?

1005. What steps can you take for positive relationships?

1006. Are there common objectives between the team and the stakeholder?

1007. What are the stakeholders interrelationships?

1008. Is access to the Issue Log controlled?

4.0 Monitoring and Controlling Process Group: Cloud Service Provider

1009. Who needs to be involved in the planning?

1010. If action is called for, what form should it take?

1011. Who needs to be engaged upfront to ensure use of results?

1012. Contingency planning. if a risk event occurs, what will you do?

1013. What input will you be required to provide the Cloud Service Provider project team?

1014. User: who wants the information and what are they interested in?

1015. Is progress on outcomes due to your program?

1016. Is it what was agreed upon?

1017. Is there undesirable impact on staff or resources?

1018. How many more potential communications channels were introduced by the discovery of the new stakeholders?

1019. How well did the team follow the chosen processes?

1020. If a risk event occurs, what will you do?

1021. Did the Cloud Service Provider project team have enough people to execute the Cloud Service Provider project plan?

1022. Where is the Risk in the Cloud Service Provider project?

1023. How do you monitor progress?

1024. Key stakeholders to work with. How many potential communications channels exist on the Cloud Service Provider project?

1025. Overall, how does the program function to serve the clients?

4.1 Project Performance Report: Cloud Service Provider

1026. What is the PRS?

1027. To what degree can the cognitive capacity of individuals accommodate the flow of information?

1028. To what degree do the structures of the formal organization motivate taskrelevant behavior and facilitate task completion?

1029. To what degree do the goals specify concrete team work products?

1030. What degree are the relative importance and priority of the goals clear to all team members?

1031. How will procurement be coordinated with other Cloud Service Provider project aspects, such as scheduling and performance reporting?

1032. Next Steps?

1033. To what degree do team members feel that the purpose of the team is important, if not exciting?

1034. To what degree are the teams goals and objectives clear, simple, and measurable?

1035. To what degree does the teams purpose constitute a broader, deeper aspiration than just accomplishing short-term goals?

1036. To what degree does the teams purpose contain themes that are particularly meaningful and memorable?

1037. To what degree do team members agree with the goals, relative importance, and the ways in which achievement will be measured?

1038. To what degree are the members clear on what they are individually responsible for and what they are jointly responsible for?

1039. To what degree are sub-teams possible or necessary?

4.2 Variance Analysis: Cloud Service Provider

1040. What was the cause of the increase in costs?

1041. Why do variances exist?

1042. Who is generally responsible for monitoring and taking action on variances?

1043. Do you identify potential or actual budget-based and time-based schedule variances?

1044. What business event caused the fluctuation?

1045. Does the contractors system provide unit or lot costs when applicable?

1046. Are work packages assigned to performing organizations?

1047. How do you evaluate the impact of schedule changes, work around, et?

1048. How does the monthly budget compare to the actual experience?

1049. Are overhead costs budgets established on a basis consistent with the anticipated direct business base?

1050. Is data disseminated to the contractors management timely, accurate, and usable?

1051. Historical experience?

1052. Contemplated overhead expenditure for each period based on the best information currently is available?

1053. How does your organization allocate the cost of shared expenses and services?

1054. Is the market likely to continue to grow at this rate next year?

1055. Are there changes in the direct base to which overhead costs are allocated?

1056. What is the actual cost of work performed?

1057. Did an existing competitor change strategy?

4.3 Earned Value Status: Cloud Service Provider

1058. Earned value can be used in almost any Cloud Service Provider project situation and in almost any Cloud Service Provider project environment. it may be used on large Cloud Service Provider projects, medium sized Cloud Service Provider projects, tiny Cloud Service Provider projects (in cut-down form), complex and simple Cloud Service Provider projects and in any market sector. some people, of course, know all about earned value, they have used it for years - but perhaps not as effectively as they could have?

1059. What is the unit of forecast value?

1060. Where is evidence-based earned value in your organization reported?

1061. When is it going to finish?

1062. Where are your problem areas?

1063. If earned value management (EVM) is so good in determining the true status of a Cloud Service Provider project and Cloud Service Provider project its completion, why is it that hardly any one uses it in information systems related Cloud Service Provider projects?

1064. How does this compare with other Cloud Service Provider projects?

1065. Validation is a process of ensuring that the developed system will actually achieve the stakeholders desired outcomes; Are you building the right product? What do you validate?

1066. How much is it going to cost by the finish?

1067. Verification is a process of ensuring that the developed system satisfies the stakeholders agreements and specifications; Are you building the product right? What do you verify?

1068. Are you hitting your Cloud Service Provider projects targets?

4.4 Risk Audit: Cloud Service Provider

1069. Are all participants informed of safety issues?

1070. What is the effect of globalisation; is business becoming too complex and can the auditor rely on auditing standards?

1071. Extending the consideration on the halo effect, to what extent are auditors able to build skepticism in evidence review?

1072. Whence the business risk audit?

1073. Does your organization have a process for meeting its ongoing taxation obligations?

1074. Do staff understand the extent of duty of care?

1075. Does your auditor understand your business?

1076. Do you have an understanding of insurance claims processes?

1077. Are some people working on multiple Cloud Service Provider projects?

1078. Assessing risk with analytical procedures: do systemsthinking tools help auditors focus on diagnostic patterns?

1079. Are end-users enthusiastically committed to the Cloud Service Provider project and the system/ product to be built?

1080. What does monitoring consist of?

1081. Is your organization an exempt employer for payroll tax purposes?

1082. Are team members trained in the use of the tools?

1083. Do your financial policies and procedures ensure that each step in financial handling (receipt, recording, banking, reporting) is not completed by one person?

1084. Do you meet all obligations relating to funds secured from grants, loans and sponsors?

1085. Are audit program plans risk-adjusted?

1086. What expertise does the Board have on quality, outcomes, and errors?

1087. Have you reviewed your constitution within the last twelve months?

4.5 Contractor Status Report: Cloud Service Provider

1088. How does the proposed individual meet each requirement?

1089. What is the average response time for answering a support call?

1090. What was the overall budget or estimated cost?

1091. How long have you been using the services?

1092. If applicable; describe your standard schedule for new software version releases. Are new software version releases included in the standard maintenance plan?

1093. Describe how often regular updates are made to the proposed solution. Are corresponding regular updates included in the standard maintenance plan?

1094. What was the final actual cost?

1095. What are the minimum and optimal bandwidth requirements for the proposed solution?

1096. Who can list a Cloud Service Provider project as organization experience, your organization or a previous employee of your organization?

1097. What was the budget or estimated cost for your organizations services?

1098. What was the actual budget or estimated cost for your organizations services?

1099. What process manages the contracts?

1100. How is risk transferred?

1101. Are there contractual transfer concerns?

4.6 Formal Acceptance: Cloud Service Provider

1102. Did the Cloud Service Provider project achieve its MOV?

1103. Did the Cloud Service Provider project manager and team act in a professional and ethical manner?

1104. Was the Cloud Service Provider project work done on time, within budget, and according to specification?

1105. Who supplies data?

1106. Was the Cloud Service Provider project managed well?

1107. What can you do better next time?

1108. What was done right?

1109. Was the client satisfied with the Cloud Service Provider project results?

1110. What function(s) does it fill or meet?

1111. Do you buy-in installation services?

1112. Have all comments been addressed?

1113. General estimate of the costs and times to complete the Cloud Service Provider project?

1114. Do you buy pre-configured systems or build your own configuration?

1115. Does it do what Cloud Service Provider project team said it would?

1116. Was the sponsor/customer satisfied?

1117. Is formal acceptance of the Cloud Service Provider project product documented and distributed?

1118. What lessons were learned about your Cloud Service Provider project management methodology?

1119. How does your team plan to obtain formal acceptance on your Cloud Service Provider project?

1120. Was business value realized?

1121. Does it do what client said it would?

5.0 Closing Process Group: Cloud Service Provider

1122. What do you need to do?

1123. What is an Encumbrance?

1124. What areas were overlooked on this Cloud Service Provider project?

1125. Is this a follow-on to a previous Cloud Service Provider project?

1126. How well did the chosen processes fit the needs of the Cloud Service Provider project?

1127. What were things that you did very well and want to do the same again on the next Cloud Service Provider project?

1128. What is the risk of failure to your organization?

1129. What will you do?

1130. Based on your Cloud Service Provider project communication management plan, what worked well?

1131. What level of risk does the proposed budget represent to the Cloud Service Provider project?

1132. Were sponsors and decision makers available when needed outside regularly scheduled meetings?

1133. Is this an updated Cloud Service Provider project Proposal Document?

1134. Were decisions made in a timely manner?

1135. What areas does the group agree are the biggest success on the Cloud Service Provider project?

1136. Did the Cloud Service Provider project team have the right skills?

1137. Did the delivered product meet the specified requirements and goals of the Cloud Service Provider project?

1138. What is the overall risk of the Cloud Service Provider project to your organization?

5.1 Procurement Audit: Cloud Service Provider

1139. How do you confirm whether the contracted organization supplied the goods or executed the work as per the quality, quantity and price indicated in the contract agreement/ supply order?

1140. If a purchase order calls for a cost-plus agreement, is the method of determining how final charges will be determined specified?

1141. Was the overall procurement done within a reasonable time?

1142. Are trial balances taken weekly for general ledgers for all funds?

1143. Is the purchasing department responsible for a continual review of marketing trends, particularly on long-term contracts and contracts containing escalation clauses?

1144. Did additional works amount to no more than 50% of the initial contract?

1145. Is it tested periodically, whether your organizations way of handling tasks is competitive in relation to price and quality?

1146. Are open purchase orders with a fixed monetary limitation used for local purchases of small dollar value?

1147. Are there reasonable procedures to identify possible sources of supply?

1148. Are reports based on sound data available to the already stated responsible for monitoring the performance of contracts?

1149. Were all admitted tenderers invited to submit a tender for each specific contract?

1150. Is an appropriated degree of standardization of goods and services respected?

1151. Has it been determined which shared services the procurement function/unit should be part of?

1152. Are proper financing arrangements taken?

1153. Was all the key documentation given to the contracting authority?

1154. Was there a sound basis for the scorings applied to the criteria and was the scoring well balanced?

1155. Are obtained prices/qualities competitive to prices/qualities obtained by other procurement functions/units, comparing obtained or improved value for money?

1156. Is confidentiality guaranteed during the whole process?

1157. Are contract changes after awarding properly justified and executed?

1158. Where required, did candidates give evidence of complying with quality assurance standards?

5.2 Contract Close-Out: Cloud Service Provider

1159. Was the contract complete without requiring numerous changes and revisions?

1160. Have all contracts been completed?

1161. Was the contract sufficiently clear so as not to result in numerous disputes and misunderstandings?

1162. Change in attitude or behavior?

1163. What is capture management?

1164. How does it work?

1165. How is the contracting office notified of the automatic contract close-out?

1166. Parties: Authorized?

1167. Have all contracts been closed?

1168. Have all acceptance criteria been met prior to final payment to contractors?

1169. How/when used ?

1170. Has each contract been audited to verify acceptance and delivery?

1171. Have all contract records been included in the

Cloud Service Provider project archives?

1172. Was the contract type appropriate?

1173. Are the signers the authorized officials?

1174. Change in knowledge?

1175. What happens to the recipient of services?

1176. Parties: who is involved?

1177. Change in circumstances?

5.3 Project or Phase Close-Out: Cloud Service Provider

1178. Planned completion date?

1179. What are they?

1180. Complete yes or no?

1181. Were cost budgets met?

1182. Were risks identified and mitigated?

1183. What were the actual outcomes?

1184. What went well?

1185. Does the lesson describe a function that would be done differently the next time?

1186. Planned remaining costs?

1187. Did the Cloud Service Provider project management methodology work?

1188. How much influence did the stakeholder have over others?

1189. What is a Risk Management Process?

1190. What was learned?

1191. Who controlled the resources for the Cloud

Service Provider project?

1192. What was expected from each stakeholder?

1193. What are the marketing communication needs for each stakeholder?

1194. What information did each stakeholder need to contribute to the Cloud Service Provider projects success?

1195. Who controlled key decisions that were made?

1196. Is there a clear cause and effect between the activity and the lesson learned?

5.4 Lessons Learned: Cloud Service Provider

1197. Is the lesson significant, valid, and applicable?

1198. What were the problems encountered in the Cloud Service Provider project-functional area relationship, why, and how could they be fixed?

1199. How complete and timely were the materials you were provided to decide whether to proceed from one Cloud Service Provider project lifecycle phase to the next?

1200. What is (are) the indicator(s) of success?

1201. What things surprised you on the Cloud Service Provider project that were not in the plan?

1202. Why does your organization need a lessons learned (LL) capability?

1203. Was the control overhead justified?

1204. How adequately involved did you feel in Cloud Service Provider project decisions?

1205. How well was Cloud Service Provider project status communicated throughout your involvement in the Cloud Service Provider project?

1206. What is the frequency of personal communications?

1207. How efficient and effective were Cloud Service Provider project team meetings?

1208. Who managed most of the communication within the Cloud Service Provider project?

1209. How comprehensive was integration testing?

1210. How was the political and social history changed over the life of the Cloud Service Provider project?

1211. How will you allocate your funding resources?

1212. What was the methodology behind successful learning experiences, and how might they be applied to the broader challenge of your organizations knowledge management?

1213. What worked well or did not work well, either for this Cloud Service Provider project or for the Cloud Service Provider project team?

1214. What policy constraints are relevant?

1215. What were the key issues?

1216. What skills did you need that were missing on this Cloud Service Provider project?

Index

311

CPSIA information can be obtained
at www.ICGtesting.com
Printed in the USA
BVHW041047100719
553067BV00013B/326/P